CONTENTS

FOREWORD

The Children Act 1989 is the most comprehensive and far reaching legislation about children and families yet enacted. Research has played a fundamental part in bringing about the changes contained in the Act. Studies carried out in the 1970s and 1980s gave a disturbing picture, individually and cumulatively, of the needs of children and the impact of social services on them and their families. The lessons of research helped to redefine the relationship between the courts, personal social services, and families and children in need.

One of the foremost social work researchers and practitioners over this period is Jane Rowe. Her work has influenced several generations of policy makers and social workers. We have been privileged in her collaboration with the Department of Health to produce firstly *Social Work Decisions in Child Care* (1985) and more recently *The Care of Children: Principles and Practice in Regulations and Guidance* (1990). With the same advisory group which assisted her in work on the Principles and Practice Guide, she has now produced a review of recent research studies focusing on the patterns and outcomes in child placements. The insights drawn from a wealth of both small and large scale studies merit detailed consideration by all social work managers and practitioners, who carry responsibility for decisions about the care of children. Moreover, these research findings reinforce the major changes which the Children Act 1989 will introduce this year.

Sir William Utting
Chief Inspector
Social Services Inspectorate

INTRODUCTION

This publication is a sequel to 'Social Work Decisions in Child Care' (HMSO 1985). Like its predecessor, it aims to make recent research findings accessible to social workers and demonstrate their relevance to day to day practice. It forms part of the Departmental publications on the Children Act 1989. (Others in the series are 'Introduction to the Children Act 1989' and 'Principles and Practice in Regulations and Guidance'.) The advisory group of experienced social work academics and practitioners which developed the principles and practice guide has produced this volume also.

Both the Act and the research findings have profound implications for policy makers, managers and practitioners, and when the Act is implemented major changes will be required, especially in relation to partnership with parents. While these legislative changes offer exciting new opportunities, they also challenge the profession's established patterns of thought and action.

The shifts in thinking which will be needed can best be achieved by making social workers fully aware of the experience and research findings which lie behind these new requirements. Social workers want what is best for the families with whom they are working. They need to be convinced that there are well founded reasons for change and that new methods and approaches will be beneficial. This is what makes the dissemination of sound research and well tested practice wisdom so essential.

The Department of Health funds a major child care research programme. In studying the patterns and outcomes of child care placements, this review draws heavily on reports commissioned by the Department but also looks wider and includes many other national and local research studies which have relevance for child care placements. However, there is no way in which a review such as this can do justice to the full range and richness of the material from all these studies. They include surveys covering hundreds or even thousands of placements while other studies consider the experiences of only a few children and families but in great depth and detail.

For this overview, the focus is on the care of those children who are being looked after by local authorities and for whom, therefore, social workers have a very special responsibility. Three themes merit particular attention. These are:

1) Promotion of the child's welfare.

2) Partnership with parents and carers.

3) Planning - both strategically and for individuals.

Some of the important topics omitted in this volume - such as disability, delinquency and child abuse - will be the subject of further work by the Department of Health. Meanwhile the better understanding of children, families and the impact of social work upon them, can flow across our artificially created boundaries to the benefit of all.

The sections which follow bring together research findings and insights applicable to the themes of promotion, partnership and planning, but there is no attempt to cover the individual research studies comprehensively. An annotated list of references is provided, but readers are urged to refer to the individual reports for further information on particular topics and to check details of definitions and samples before attempting to apply research findings to an individual case.

The cumulative effect of research reports is weighty and powerful and it is folly to ignore the messages from well conducted research studies. However, it is also important to remember that research has to deal with generalities, whereas, in child care, decisions must be taken about individuals. Research can provide essential background but cannot substitute for detailed knowledge of a particular child and family. Thus research cannot take the place of carefully collected evidence or professional judgement, but it can provide a solid basis on which sound judgements and good practice can develop. The working party believes that, if they are taken in conjunction with basic child care principles, the findings reported here can enhance the professional judgement of policy makers, managers and practitioners and will help in the development of higher standards.

One of the crucial messages which emerges from prolonged study of a whole series of child care research reports is the importance of adequate and accurate evidence. The 'exercises' or 'tools for practice' included at the end of this volume have therefore been designed to provide an opportunity for social workers and their managers to develop some new ways of gathering, analysing and weighing up the evidence upon which services should be planned and decisions for individual children should be made.

MEMBERS OF THE ADVISORY GROUP

Wendy Rose (*In the chair*)	Assistant Chief Inspector Social Services Inspectorate Department of Health
Jane Rowe OBE	Child Care Researcher Project Consultant
Dr Jane Aldgate	Lecturer and Fellow of St Hilda's College, Oxford
Dr Carolyn Davies	Principal Research Officer Department of Health
Philip Douglas	Operations Manager Northamptonshire County Council Social Services Department
John Fitzgerald OBE	Director The Bridge Child Care Consultancy Service
Geoff Gildersleeve	Social Services Inspector Department of Health
John Goldup	Family Services Manager London Borough of Islington Social Services Department
Jeff Hopkins	Lecturer Department of Applied Social Studies and Social Work Keele University
Brother James	Catholic Child Welfare Society Diocese of Middlesbrough
Geoffrey James	Social Services Inspector Department of Health
Jim Kennedy	Social Services Inspector Department of Health
Barbara K Lerner	Development Officer Hertfordshire County Council Social Services Department
Ruth Prime	Social Services Inspector Department of Health

Paul Sutton   Director
                   Birmingham Action on Child Care
                   City of Birmingham
                   Social Services Department

June Thoburn   Senior Lecturer
                   University of East Anglia

PART ONE PROMOTION OF THE CHILD'S WELFARE

The Children Act 1989 places a strong emphasis on identifying and meeting the needs of children. It goes further than earlier legislation in spelling out those aspects of children's lives which are essential to their welfare and which must therefore be taken into consideration when decisions are made. Racial origin, culture and linguistic background take their place with age and religion as relevant factors; issues about contact with parents, relatives and friends are now set alongside more traditional issues about where and with whom a child should live. 'Family' is interpreted in its widest sense to include not only blood relatives but others who are important because the child has been living with them or because they have parental responsibility.

Promotion of welfare naturally includes protection from harm, but it is also widened to cover all aspects of children's health and development and though the Act does not specifically use the words 'identity' or 'achievement of potential', these concepts are clearly implied.

The known difficulties for authorities in acting corporately as a good parent are indirectly addressed by the Act in its stress on preserving children's birth families whenever possible by maintaining continuity of family relationships and responsibilities. There is also additional emphasis on authorities' duties to assist and befriend young people whom they have previously looked after.* These matters are supported and illuminated by research findings which are grouped into three sub-sections:

1) Meeting needs and developing potential; early disadvantage and making up deficits; moving into independence; ethnic minorities.

2) The importance of maintaining the child's own home.

3) Family links with emphasis on siblings.

---

*When possible, the new terminology of the Children Act 1989 has been used in this document. For example, the old phrases 'being in care', or 'admitted to care' become 'being looked after by the local authority' and 'admitted to care or accommodation', while 'home on trial' becomes 'placement at home'. However, when direct reference is being made to the findings of pre-1989 research, it is necessary to revert to the earlier terminology because this is what was in use at the time the studies were conducted and the reports on them were written.

1 Meeting Needs and Developing Potential

a) Children and young people who need placement are already disadvantaged

'Deprivation is a common factor among all types of children who enter care' (Bebbington and Miles 1989). In a study of 2,500 children admitted to care these researchers found that before admission:

- only a quarter were living with both parents;

- almost three-quarters of their families received income support;

- only one in five lived in owner occupied housing;

- over one half were living in 'poor' neighbourhoods.

Other factors creating greater likelihood of admission were overcrowding (linked with large families); young mothers; and a child's parents being of different racial origins. The cumulative effect of these factors shows up starkly in two tables in the Bebbington and Miles report which compare the probability of admission for two children of similar age but in very different circumstances.

Child 'A'	Child 'B'
Aged 5 to 9	Aged 5 to 9
No dependence on social security benefits	Household head receives income support
Two parent family	Single adult household
Three or fewer children	Four or more children
White	Mixed ethnic origin
Owner occupied home	Privately rented home
More rooms than people	One or more persons per room
Odds are 1 in 7,000	*Odds are 1 in 10*

These researchers found that deprivation was even more closely associated with coming into care in the 1980s than it was in the 1962 study by Packman. However, offenders were rather less likely to come from severely deprived households and more often came from intact families. (This finding is supported by Farmer and Parker 1989). In Bebbington and Miles' view it is probably not only the poverty of single parents but also their lack of available social supports which makes their children more liable to need looking after away from home. They also draw attention to the interaction of environmental problems or disability and family stress and breakdown.

Studying reasons for admission to care in Essex, Wedge and Phelan (1987) found that social workers cited disrupted family relationships as a contributory factor in over half of all admissions, and Bebbington and Miles note that 'broken family' had replaced unemployment as the factor most highly correlated with entry into care. The parents' own deprivation or ill-health were each mentioned as contributing to about 15% of Essex admissions, but it was noteworthy that social workers seldom mentioned low income, poor housing, unemployment or cultural difficulties as contributory factors (one can only speculate that perhaps they took this for granted). Stone's recent (1990) study of short-term fostering in Newcastle reports that social workers considered that three-fifths of the children of all ages in her sample had experienced abuse or neglect at some time.

b) The need to remedy these disadvantages

Because of their material and emotional deprivations, children tend to enter the public care system with problems of health, development and behaviour and with educational deficits. There has been a dearth of research evidence on these topics which is only gradually being rectified. Such data as are available have been helpfully summarised by Kahan (1989) and Jackson (1987) in papers on the health and education of children in care. Both paint a disturbing picture which highlights the importance of the Children Act's emphasis on meeting needs and helping children to achieve a reasonable standard of health and development. It is salutary to reflect that far from remedying existing deficiencies, research is showing that periods in public care have further impaired the life chances of some children and young people because of poor educational achievement, uncorrected health problems and maladjustment.

Health problems of children in care and lack of emphasis on health needs were cited by the House of Commons Social Services Committee in 1983–4. This led the Economic and Social Research Council to commission papers from Dr Frank Bamford and Dr Stephen Wolkind (1988). They concluded that those who had been in care were gravely disadvantaged as a group with higher risks of psychiatric ill health and social deviance than any other easily identified group in our society.

Some reasons for this unsatisfactory state of affairs emerged from the Social Services Committee's enquiries and the Bamford and Wolkind reports, though specific research to confirm these judgements is still lacking. Identified problems include:

1) The child in care may not have any one person who is intimately familiar with her/his history, or alert to symptoms which an ordinary parent would notice. A telling example from Dr Wolkind is that 'it is very easy for children to go through care with no one knowing whether they are right-handed or left-handed'.

2) Medical examinations of children on admission and during foster home placements are undervalued and often overlooked. They may also fail to provide relevant information.

3) Medical histories of children in care are usually 'grossly inadequate' and seldom include an interview with the parents.

4) The value and importance of growth charts in assessing a child's overall well-being are not yet sufficiently recognised for children being looked after by local authorities even though this was pointed out by the Maria Colwell Report as long ago as 1973.

5) Little use has so far been made of the large amount of data potentially available from analysis of medical records.

Evidence on the education of children in care is also thin. This is itself a sign of the low priority that education has been given in the care system. Another is that few young people leave care with any academic qualifications, while community homes providing education on the premises have been heavily criticised for poor standards (DES 1980). Triseliotis and Russell (1984) found that adopted children were more likely to achieve well in school than those brought up in residential establishments but both these groups were significantly more likely than long-term foster children to remain in school beyond the statutory leaving age.

Jackson comments that social workers may have been insufficiently aware of links between social and psychological adjustment and school achievement and between educational achievement and satisfying, well-paid employment. They also tended to have low expectations of educational achievement for children in care. Berridge and Cleaver (1987) join Jackson in pointing out that the effect of damaging discontinuities of schooling seems to receive rather little attention from decision makers, and the SSI review of local authority policy statements (Robbins 1990) notes that 'the health and educational needs of children in care and their future employment prospects are tackled relatively rarely'.

Lack of concern over education was also noted in Farmer and Parker's report on 'home on trial' placements. Well over half of the adolescents at 'home on trial' had poor school attendance but their social workers did not take this too seriously and liaison with schools was limited both before and during 'home on trial' placements.

Research is now clarifying two important themes. The first is that just being in care is not usually in itself a primary cause of educational failure. It is rather that children bring their educational problems with them into care and too often the care experience does little to ameliorate these deficiencies. Heath, Colton and Aldgate (1989) have shown that the below average attainments of children in long and medium stay foster homes were no worse than those of a control group of children receiving social services help in their own homes. But if their foster care experience had not lowered their attainment levels, nor had it improved them. Some explanation of their findings is emerging from a current study by Aldgate and Heath (Aldgate 1990). This is showing that a sense of permanence is a crucial element in determining school achievement. Support for this theory comes from Garnett (1989) who reports that those who have grown up in care have slightly higher educational attainments than those who enter care in adolescence *especially if they have been in a settled placement.*

c) The practical problems and personal deficits of young people moving into independence

Leaving care for independence is a crisis which brings to the surface past deficits in care and attainment; it often requires, but does not receive, a major input of services and support. Recent studies of care leavers present some reliable data on the condition and experiences of young people leaving care to live independently. Stein and Carey's (1986) interviews with young people provide vivid insights into their feelings, attitudes and experiences. As one of them remarked: 'It's not being in care. What matters is when you've got to leave it. Where are you gonna be? Where are you gonna go? What's gonna happen?' A similar sentiment was expressed by a young care leaver who was interviewed by Bonnerjea (1990). He said: 'Being in care is a game. It's when you get out that it's real.'

Garnett has gathered detailed and factual information on a group of care leavers from three authorities and discusses the services available or still needed, while Bonnerjea reports on provision for care leavers in the London boroughs. Both draw urgent attention to the gulf between the current position and what is really required. The Children Act 1989 lays a duty upon local authorities to provide preparation for leaving care and to 'advise, assist and befriend' care leavers aged 16-21. The same section of the Act authorises, but does not require, the giving of assistance 'in kind, or in exceptional circumstances, in cash'. Meeting even these modest targets will make major demands on social work time.

Garnett says:

> 'Although we cannot be certain of how typical our three study authorities are, they do illustrate just how basic current services are within some local authority departments. For example, not one of our three authorities had developed formal plans for the preparation and after care of these young people. There were no 'leaving-care' budgets, and few if any written guidelines on how social workers, residential staff or foster parents might proceed in preparing and supporting young people leaving their charge.'

In London in 1989, Bonnerjea found that only half the boroughs provided independence training in their children's homes. There seemed to be little concern about the appropriate content of such training and little effort was being put into developing it. Not surprisingly, the young people who had been on the receiving end were quite critical and disillusioned about what was provided. The proportion of boroughs with specific leaving care schemes was even smaller - only 13 out of 33.

Of course, not all care leavers require intensive help from field or residential social workers. Some leave care from long-term foster homes in which they have a secure base. However, Garnett found that these formed only about 20% of care leavers. Another 20% were long-term care cases but had no stable base from which to launch into independence while the majority (60%) had entered care in their teens. The less clearly defined groups in the Stein and Carey study followed a similar pattern.

Reference has already been made to these young people's lack of educational qualifications and both the Garnett and the Stein and Carey studies showed that few complete any further training. Their employment opportunities were diminished by this and the research shows the proportion of care leavers without jobs is consistently higher than the local average. A further cause for concern is Garnett's finding that one in seven of the girls leaving care at 18 was already pregnant.

Access to accommodation is obviously an issue of major importance to those whose period of being looked after by the local authority is ending. There is wide variation between authorities in terms of available housing, links between social services and housing departments and provision by voluntary organisations. However, several clear messages come through from various studies and reports:

1) Even if not actually without a roof over their heads, care leavers quite often experience periods of 'semi-homelessness', frequent moves between shoddy bedsits, shared flats, squatting, staying with friends and relatives (Partridge 1989).

2) The ex-care population has been found to be heavily over-represented in the group of homeless and often destitute young people now to be found in London and some other major cities (Centrepoint report quoted by Hardwick 1989).

3) Even when young people obtain the tenancy of a flat, they often find themselves lonely and unable to cope on their very limited finances so that debts accumulate. Out of 15 young people previously in care whose last placement was a flat and whose whereabouts were known two years later, only three were still living there (Garnett).

4) To be fully effective, specialist preparation for independence units must have access to suitable permanent

accommodation. Not all of them have this and Garnett states bluntly: 'Any benefits that might be gained from these placements will be cancelled out if young people are forced to move on, ready or not, to temporary and unsuitable living arrangements at 17 or 18 years of age.'

There is evidence from all the studies of care leavers that discharge to 'independence' is occurring at increasingly younger ages. Bonnerjea states that policies of flexibility about the age for leaving care seemed to result in authorities encouraging youngsters to leave residential accommodation early. Stein and Carey question the stress on independence and urge the concept of inter-dependence. They point out that in the general population only 0.5% of 16-17 year olds live alone, yet 'a group of young people regarded as being in need of care and control up to the age of sixteen, seventeen or eighteen are catapulted into a position of greater vulnerability than that of other people their age'.

The well-being of young care leavers depends not just on practical matters such as housing and employment, vital though these are. In an unpublished study, 'Growing Up Alone', Sarah Wedge (1988) explores the role of parents, relatives and friends as adolescents seek to achieve independence and struggle with problems of identity and autonomy. She also considers the difficulties created for adolescents who were being looked after by local authorities because of the division of responsibility between parents, carers and local authority staff, and the discontinuities of relationships which resulted from admission to care, from placement changes and staff turnover. It is a useful, if salutary, exercise to consider what relationships and resources are available to each young person moving into independent living arrangements. What links do they have with parents, siblings, other relatives? With past carers and social workers? With peers? With people in the community? To whom can they turn for emotional support, for advice or companionship?

Although Robbins reports that two-thirds of the local authority policy statements she studied made reference to the need to prepare young people for independence, it appears that 'outreach' after-care services were usually very limited. Partridge found that 'young people experienced very polarised support systems when they left care. Either they had established a close relationship with a caring figure or there was nothing.' Garnett says: 'Two-thirds of our sample had no specific contact plans, the most common arrangement being for young people to come back on their own initiative if and when they needed help.' In some instances the care leavers were thought to have adequate support, in others to be unwilling to accept it. Sometimes the young person had already lost touch with the department even before formal discharge.

An interesting finding of this and other leaving care studies is that a substantial proportion - more than one in three - did come back for further help. This finding is supported by Stein and Carey and by Bonnerjea who noted that a number of those who wanted nothing more to do with social services when they first left care, later felt a great need for support as they struggled to establish themselves as independent adults. These delayed calls for help can create both practical and policy problems for departments. Staff changes, closure of residential establishments and the young people's moves across team boundaries can mean that familiar workers are no longer available. But there have also been questions about who should be responsible and whether these young people should be considered continuing child care cases or treated like any other young adult seeking help from social services. If the latter option was chosen, the 'help' given was likely to be referral on to housing departments, social security or local voluntary organisations. Section 24 of the Children Act 1989 has now made it clear that young people under 21 who have been looked after by a local authority after the age of 16 will qualify for special advice and assistance.

The main issue over implementing this part of the Act is likely to be the amount of social work time needed to fulfil the advising and befriending duties. Bonnerjea offers a tentative estimate that provision of a minimum service for 100 care leavers would require 560 hours of direct contacts and a similar amount of time for development work in the community. Management and evaluation are estimated as needing about 380 hours, making a total of 1,500 hours. Although it is only about 40 weeks' work to service 100 care leavers, this is far in excess of what is currently available.

d) Children from minority ethnic groups

The new Children Act requires consideration of a child's racial origin and culture. However, recent research reports do not provide many suggestions about how this is to be put into effect. Indeed, in many of them ethnic issues are not addressed. None offers data on the dominant issue of whether children must *always* be placed with families of the same racial background. This indicates the need for future research to give special attention to the issues involved in identifying and meeting the needs of children from minority ethnic groups. At present only a few authorities have more than token specialist provision for black children. For instance, so far, only six out of 33 London boroughs have any special services for black care leavers (Bonnerjea).

If departments do not even know how many children from black and minority ethnic groups they are looking after, or their cultural and linguistic background, it is most unlikely that they will be able to provide appropriately for them. As the House of Commons Social Services Committee pointed out in 1984, it is difficult to analyse problems of minority ethnic children or plan to meet their needs 'if the simplest facts are not available'. There are still no national and few local authority figures on ethnicity, but recent research does begin to offer a somewhat clearer picture of patterns of admissions and discharges of children from different ethnic minorities. A complicating factor is that major differences in the ethnic mix of populations - even in neighbouring authorities - means that research findings on proportions of children from minority groups cannot be transferred from one authority to another. Probably this also accounts for what may sometimes appear to be contradictory research findings.

In 'Child Care Now', Rowe et al (1989) explain how, within the overall group of children from minority ethnic groups, there are major differences in admission rates. They also explode the myth that teenage admissions are heavily weighted with black youngsters. They report:

> 'Black children were over-represented in admissions to care of all six project authorities, although the extent to which this was happening varied considerably. Equally important are the marked differences between the minority groups . . . Asian children were under-represented in all age groups . . . African and Afro-Caribbean children were over-represented particularly in the pre-school and five to ten groups where their admission rates were more than twice that of white

children. African teenagers continued to be over-represented . . . but Afro-Caribbean teenagers entered care at only slightly higher rates than their white contemporaries.'

But the most outstanding finding about minority ethnic children in public care is the grossly disproportionate number of those of mixed racial parentage. Bebbington and Miles calculated that such children were two and a half times as likely to enter care as white children, all other things being equal. Looking at just one London borough, Barn (1990) found that Afro-Caribbean children predominated, but Rowe et al report a similar pattern to Bebbington and Miles and show that children of mixed parentage were much the largest sub-group of all the black children being looked after by the local authorities in their sample.

> *'(There was) a remarkably high overall admission rate for children of mixed parentage . . . in all age groups but particularly amongst pre-schoolers . . . When the authorities' figures for admission of mixed parentage children are examined individually, interesting differences can be seen. In areas with large black populations . . . mixed parentage children accounted for less than half of black admissions to care. But in authorities where black people account for a smaller proportion of the population, the majority of black children admitted to care proved to be those of mixed parentage.'*

Young children of mixed parentage are also the most likely to have multiple admissions. Their re-admission rate was more than twice that of young white children in the 'Child Care Now' sample and the implications are that an alarmingly large proportion of youngsters who have one white and one black or minority ethnic parent will experience multiple admissions during their childhood.

The very small number of Asian children who need care outside their family network is worthy of further enquiry. It may be that the strength of the extended family and community support makes public care less necessary, but it could be that child care services are not offered in a way acceptable to Asian parents. This is an example of the effect of cultural differences on family relationships and an indication of the need for further attention to cultural issues.

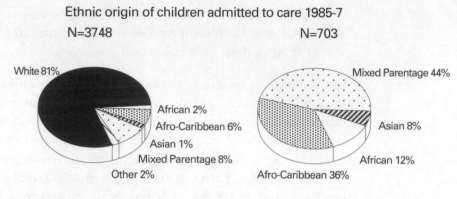

Ethnic origin of children admitted to care 1985-7

N=3748   N=703

White 81%

African 2%
Afro-Caribbean 6%
Asian 1%
Mixed Parentage 8%
Other 2%

Mixed Parentage 44%
Asian 8%
African 12%
Afro-Caribbean 36%

(From Rowe et al. 'Child Care Now')

Survey data such as those available from 'Child Care Now' are of limited help when it comes to care experiences and placement outcomes for black children, but they do offer some basic facts and dispel some misperceptions. The most useful and interesting findings are:

1) Fewer black than white children are admitted for long-term care but children of mixed parentage are more like white children in this respect.

2) Admissions with the aim of 'temporary care' are much more common for young Afro-Caribbean and African children than for any other group. In the two London boroughs in the 'Child Care Now' sample, black children accounted for 48% and 61% of all temporary care admissions of pre-school and primary school children. This is a much higher proportion than would be expected on the basis of population and clearly has important implications for foster family recruitment.

3) There are fewer compulsory admissions of black children.

4) There are only minor differences between ethnic groups in length of time in care. Afro-Caribbean and African pre-schoolers very seldom have long stays but adolescents in these groups do seem rather more likely to remain for longer periods than white adolescents.

5) Placement patterns are remarkably similar for all ethnic groups and in 'Child Care Now' fostering rates are reported as almost identical though Knapp (1988) found that in the authority he studied, black boys were less likely to be fostered than white boys.

(6)   Ethnicity seems to have little to do with placement outcome
       or 'success' rates if success is equated with lasting. The
       proportion of placements which did not last as needed was
       virtually identical across all ethnic groups in the 'Child Care
       Now' sample and in a survey of permanent placements by
       Thoburn and Rowe (1988) and in Fratter et al (1991). In this
       latter survey, however, being of mixed parentage was more
       likely to be associated with breakdown. When both parents
       were black or from minority ethnic groups, the children
       were more likely than either white children or those of
       mixed parentage to have remained in contact with their birth
       families.

Beyond and behind these surface findings come some disturbing
glimpses of problems of black children and young people being
looked after in a largely white oriented care system. A quote
from Stein and Carey's 'Leaving Care' once again gives the
flavour of a young person's feelings:

> *'Here I am in a black community. I've grown up 'white' but
> they can't see. Which do I turn to - white or black? I daren't
> step forward, I can't step back. Help me someone please to find
> my culture and identity. Why could I not have these when I
> was young? They brought me up to think being black is
> wrong.'*

Another reminder of the improved awareness, knowledge and
resources that will be needed to carry forward the Children Act's
aims for minority ethnic children comes from Partridge. She
quotes a staff member's proud statement: 'Our black children
leave here feeling they're white.'

The future challenge for social workers and managers will be to
move from rhetoric or lip service to action. Racial and ethnic
issues must be raised to their proper place alongside those of
culture, class and gender without ignoring, exaggerating or
distorting any of these essential elements in each child's
individuality and personal history.

2 The Importance of Maintaining the Child's Own Home

a) The risk of instability in long-term care

Research on a range of topics shows how difficult it is to provide a stable and positive experience for children or young people who are being looked after by local authorities for more than a brief period.

Premature endings and placement change continue to be prevalent. In 'Child Care Now', Rowe et al report that nearly a quarter of all placements failed to last as long as needed and a third did not last as long as planned. Offenders entering care in their early to mid-adolescence were found to have the most moves, especially those who were on criminal care orders, and it seems clear that a relatively small group of young people accounted for a large number of placements. However, this study reinforces previous reports that in all age groups there are some children who experience an unacceptably large number of moves.

Although the early months after admission see the most moves, stability is not readily achieved later. In Garnett's study of young people leaving care for independence, only half of those who had come into care before their teen years were able to leave care from a stable, long-term placement, and in their study of care leavers, Stein and Carey found that 40% of them had had five or more placements during their care career.

Changes of placement may be due to crisis admissions, to breakdowns and to unforeseen circumstances, but changes also occur for administrative convenience or as part of the planning process. Berridge (1985) puts the proportion of 'administrative' moves at two-thirds and Garnett describes the 'staged nature' of much of the move-on accommodation provided for young people preparing for independent living.

Research is now beginning to help differentiate between the effects of short, intermediate and long-term arrangements by social agencies for looking after children.

1) **Short-term**. Studies by Packman and by Fisher et al (1986) show that most parents and children who experienced relatively brief periods of care felt that it achieved some benefits for them. Even if nothing else was done, care which was provided during a family crisis helped to solve the immediate problem or offered much needed relief. Findings

from 'Child Care Now' show that placements with the aim of 'temporary care' almost always achieved this aim.

2) **Medium-term**. Arrangements for intermediate length periods are usually intended to achieve some specific purpose involving changes in behaviour, relationships or family circumstances. 'Child Care Now' examined individual placement outcomes rather than care episode outcomes, but its findings on the relative lack of success in achieving such placement aims as 'treatment of child and/or family', 'bridge to independence' or 'assessment' indicate the difficulty of providing effective care for children and families who may have had many, and often long-standing, personal and environmental problems. Nevertheless, a period of several years of being looked after by the local authority may be the best option for certain children and young people and achieve positive, if imperfect, results.

3) **Long-term**. Several researchers have found that having had an extended stay in care is negatively associated with placement outcome. Thus Farmer and Parker found that 'the more disrupted and longer the period in care before the child goes home on trial, the greater the difficulties are likely to be'. Both Wedge and Mantle and Rushton et al (1989) found a similar pattern in permanent substitute family placements and Berridge and Cleaver came to the same conclusion in their study of foster family care.

In spite of the strong evidence on the difficulties of providing stable long-term arrangements, there is another side to the coin which needs to be borne in mind when decisions are being made. As Millham and colleagues in the Dartington Research Unit (1986) and also Farmer and Parker point out, 'return home' is all too likely to mean returning to a changed household. For example, while the departure of the perpetrator of previous abuse may be beneficial, a loved parent may now be absent and the introduction of step-parents, co-habitees and new children is often a cause of stress. Too hasty a return home can be counter-productive and may result in re-admission, while if continuity can be achieved by a 'permanent' fostering or adoptive placement which lasts, long-term outcomes are generally positive. Breakdowns of long-term placements continue to be a cause for concern but both Triseliotis (1989) and Thoburn (1990) have shown that most young people who have grown up in stable family placements speak warmly of their experiences even when some problems have persisted.

b) The leaving care curve

If lengthy stays away from home are to be avoided, efforts to re-establish the family and promote necessary changes are obviously essential. Research now highlights the speed at which this needs to be done.

Researchers have now established beyond doubt that there is a leaving curve which slopes up very sharply at first and then abruptly flattens out. Whereas it used to be thought that children who were still in care after a few months were likely to remain a long time, it is now clear that it is a matter of weeks not months. *Most of those who remain after six weeks are destined for a long or very long stay.* About one child in three leaves in less than a month and almost half have gone by six months. But after that discharges slow to a trickle and about one child in three remains for more than a year. (The Dartington studies, 'Child Care Now', Wedge and Phelan in Essex and Thorpe's work in Leicestershire all show a similar patttern.)

If the welfare of long stay children is to be properly promoted, it is first necessary to identify them. Recent studies show that they fall into two main groups whose needs are rather different. Some will have been admitted while still very young but the majority of 'stayers' enter the care system in their early teens and remain for several years. Garnett's study of young people leaving care for independence shows that 40% had been in care a very long time but 60% had been admitted in their teens.

The legal route at entry to care has been strongly associated with length of stay, with children and young people admitted on court orders being twice as likely to stay in care a long time. However, it is important to recognise that this is an association not necessarily a cause. It does seem likely that, for a whole variety of reasons, the making of a court order has an independent effect on length of stay. But since it is those cases which present the most difficult and deep seated problems which are the most likely to be brought to a court, they are the cases where a lengthy stay is most probable no matter what the legal status. The new Children Act strongly supports avoidance of compulsion, but simply choosing the voluntary route will not in itself guarantee a shorter stay. Positive action is required to achieve rapid and successful restoration home.

The Children Act seeks to remove the stigma that became attached even to voluntary admissions to care and puts forward the provision of 'accommodation' for children in need as a means of sustaining family functioning. 'Accommodation' is clearly intended to function more like the current use of respite care for children with disabilities under pre-1989 arrangements.

The evidence from 'Child Care Now' is that a few authorities have already started to use short-term care/'accommodation' in this way but most have not. Several studies noted that re-admissions to care were common, but they were usually caused by further family crises and breakdowns and were not part of planned family support. A special follow-up of the original Dartington cohort showed that within two years of discharge, 22% had been re-admitted at least once and a further 6% had three or more re-admissions. This figure is replicated in 'Child Care Now' which also notes that an astonishing 49% of children admitted between the ages of 5-10 had experienced at least one previous admission. So had 38% of adolescents. Stone's study of short-stay fostering in Newcastle also found that the majority of school age children coming into placement had embarked on their career in care when they were younger.

Little is known about what proportion of those re-admitted are able to return to the same placement as they were in on previous occasions, though Farmer and Parker found that of those where 'home on trial' placements broke down, only about one in five was able to go back to the same foster home or residential establishment. Nor is there as yet any substantive body of research on the effect of multiple separations for the purpose of relief. In the light of the Act's emphasis on the provision of accommodation as a means of preserving families under stress, this is clearly a serious gap in our knowledge. A study by Stalker (1990) of family based respite care for children with learning difficulties in Lothian concludes that in spite of some distress and homesickness, the majority of children enjoyed and benefited from their respite placements. (Children always went to the same carers). Most parents also benefited, but Stalker comments that socially disadvantaged families had difficulties in making use of the scheme, which could not provide sufficient help where coping strategies had all but broken down, and the real need was for long-term placement.

c) Birth families provide continuity, roots and identity

Even when birth families are marginalised by the care process, they remain an important source of continuity. The powerful psychological influence of the 'hidden', internalised parent has been known for many decades even if it is not always remembered and appreciated. Now, the Dartington researchers have pointed out that frequent changes of placement and social worker mean that the birth family may in fact be the most stable influence in the child's experience even if actual contact is very limited.

British research has also replicated studies by Fanshel and Shinn (1978) in the United States which showed that family contact is the 'key to discharge'. This message is clearly a crucial one for practitioners. In their detailed study of family links, the Dartington research unit made it clear that while links did not ensure exit from care, children who became cut off from their family of origin were likely to stay indefinitely even though they might have improved in health, behaviour and functioning (Millham et al).

Evidence from a number of studies shows that no matter if family links have been weak, or turbulent, most children and young people who experience care do return to their parents or at least to some member of their family. Those who graduate from care at 18 may re-establish links and benefit from support, even if living independently (Stein and Carey), and the wider family network may provide at least a temporary roof when other living arrangements fail (Farmer and Parker).

The need for knowledge of one's origins has been highlighted by research which has monitored new legislation on access to birth records by adoptees (Haimes and Timms 1989 and Howe and Hinings 1989), and by texts such as Rockel and Ryburn's 'Adoption Today' (1988). The messages from these adoption studies have equal relevance for young people in long-term care or accommodation and help to broaden the concept of links beyond face to face visits (which may not be possible or desirable under all circumstances) to include other forms of contact, information and background histories, and the preservation of links which permit contact to be resumed at a later date if desired.

In the early days of what has become known as 'the permanence movement', the emphasis was largely on achieving security through adoption. Continuing parental access was seen as a bar to this. More recently, practitioners and researchers have questioned the need for children to lose all their family links in order to gain security. Thoburn (1988) has clarified the various routes to permanence and in doing this enlarged our concepts of both adoption and foster care. A small scale study by Fratter (1989) and Fratter et al (1991) explored access in permanent placements and concludes that 'a child's need for contact does not necessarily conflict with the achievement of permanence and a secure placement can be offered to children through permanent foster care'.

3 Family Links and Sibling Relationships

a) Contact and placement stability

By the mid-1980s there was cumulative research evidence from both the USA and Great Britain showing that the well being of children being cared for by social agencies is enhanced if they maintain links with parents and other family members. Unfortunately, other research showed that all too often links were not being maintained. In the second half of the decade, both sets of messages have been confirmed and the Children Act not only makes new requirements on local authorities to actively promote links, but also changes the terminology and broadens the concept of 'access' to one of 'contact'. This includes links of all kinds from visits to telephone calls and presents.

Berridge and Cleaver found that frequent access to parents was associated with fewer fostering breakdowns. Thoburn and Rowe's adoption survey showed that when other variables were held constant, few placements broke down when family links were maintained, while Wedge and Mantle discovered that even among a group of children who were being placed in permanent substitute families, those whose links with their birth families had been maintained were protected against the adverse effects of long periods in care. They noted that 50% of children referred for permanent placement had some link with their birth family at that time. They tended to be older children who presumably could maintain links themselves. These researchers conclude: 'The increasing trend towards access of family members to children in care needs to be further developed and extended if placements in substitute families are to be as successful as possible and if children are to acquire and retain the self-identity which is a crucial component in healthy emotional development.'

The findings, insights and conclusions from the Dartington Research Unit's study 'Lost in Care' (1986) are admirably summarised in their follow-up research 'Access Disputes in Child Care' (1989). They are sufficiently important to require quoting at some length:

> '*On a child's entry to care, the social worker has to decide where the child should be placed, the implications of the legal status, how long the child is likely to be away and what kinds of access arrangements should be made for parents. Managing a crisis, finding a suitable placement, coping with the anxiety,*

grief and frequent hostility of parents and children make it difficult for social workers to give the maintenance of links between parents and absent children high priority. Contacts are left to emerge, consequent upon other social worker decisions.

As a result, withering links with home affect many children in care; from the outset, nearly three-quarters of children experience great difficulty in maintaining contact with their parents. The barriers that they face are of two kinds. The first are specific restrictions, which are placed by social workers on the access of individuals, usually family or other household members. Such difficulties affect one-third of the children on entry. The second barrier is created by non-specific restrictions, difficulties inherent in placements, such as hostility, distance and inaccessibility. These hindrances affect two-thirds of the children in the early days of care.

As time passes, child isolation increases and restrictions on parental access to children actually increase, often to help maintain placements in difficulty, although the disruptive potential of visiting parents is over-estimated. Restrictions on contact do not receive continual scrutiny by social workers and constraints on unwelcome family members are frequently allowed to linger long after the original reasons for discouraging visits have evaporated. In addition, non-specific barriers to contact, those that are inherent in distance, routine, rules and inaccessibility of placements, remain pressing, often aggravated by movements of children between placements.

Other factors increase the child's isolation. Social workers' visits to parents, children and care givers decline over time. We found that, by the end of two years, one-third of the mothers, nearly all of the fathers and half of the children in care were receiving infrequent visits from social workers. Thus, the bridge between absent child and his or her family weakens and the social worker fails to stress the significance of parent/child reciprocal contact. Unfortunately, parents need encouragement to maintain relationships with their absent children, particularly when haunted by a sense of failure and bereft of a useful role.

The implications of these difficulties are severe. If children remain in care for two years or more and away from home, four-fifths of them will experience severe barriers to maintaining contact with their parents and nearly half will have access restrictions still imposed on some adult, usually a family member. In addition, almost all will have other pressing barriers to contact. As a result, a third of those who remain in care will have lost contact with mother or father, siblings or the wider family at the end of two years and will be likely to stay in care for the foreseeable future. In the majority of cases, there are no cogent social work reasons for contacts with the family to wither. Indeed, good practice should have nurtured family links because it is to home and neighbourhood most children return on leaving care.'

The Dartington team's work on access disputes disclosed a national picture of about a thousand formal termination of access notices being given each year but unevenly spread across the authorities. In addition the researchers calculate that there are twice as many instances of 'de facto' terminations where parents are effectively squeezed out of the picture or themselves fail to maintain or press for access. The children involved tend to be young and their families are particularly disadvantaged and disorganised even in comparison with others in the care system.

An especially worrying finding is that access to family may be terminated before any settled and secure placement is in sight. Indeed, a quarter of the children in the sample were seen by their social workers as likely to be living independently at 18 years of age and largely bereft of adult support. Premature termination of access may well do the child a serious disservice because it precludes the possibility of retaining contact while still achieving a secure family placement.

Although Wedge and Mantle speak of 'the increasing trend' toward access, other researchers point out the low base from which this trend is starting. Thoburn's intensive and extensive studies of 'permanent' placements both show that family links which children wished to maintain were not always preserved, and in their studies of fostering breakdown Berridge and Cleaver noted an 'anti-family ideology' in some instances and more general lack of encouragement of contact, which meant that family links were too often allowed to wither and die.

The use of relations as a placement resource has received little attention until the last few years and has sometimes been frowned on as likely to exacerbate family tensions. However, if children's parents are unable or unwilling to care for them, an obvious way to preserve close links is to turn to the wider family, and the high level of stability and satisfaction found in foster placements with relatives which was first emphasised in 'Long-Term Foster Care' (Rowe et al 1984) has been strongly reinforced in recent studies. The benefits of maintaining family links through placement with relatives comes through strongly in a recent study of custodianship (Malos and Bullard 1990).

In 'Foster Home Breakdown' Berridge and Cleaver report a remarkable success rate for fostering by relatives and in 'Child Care Now' Rowe et al report that relatives tend to foster older children with more complex problems and still achieve better results than unrelated foster carers. Despite this, local authorities vary greatly in their use of fostering by relatives and their willingness to provide financial support for people looking after relatives' children.

Farmer and Parker point out that although only a small proportion of 'home on trial' placements were made with relatives, the wider family were sometimes brought into the picture and provided valuable support if the first home on trial placement with parent(s) did not work out.

b) Sibling relationships merit closer attention

Research underlies and supports the requirement in the Children Act 1989 (S23(7)(b)) that siblings should be accommodated together whenever 'reasonably practicable and consistent with the child's welfare'. Psychologists such as Judy Dunn point out that siblings provide our longest lasting relationships and can be a powerful influence on personality and development.

However, this explicit attention to the question of siblings is relatively recent and there are few references to siblings in local authority policy documents or practice guides.

Between a third and a half of all admissions to care or accommodation involve sibling groups but there are wide variations by age and circumstances. Those admitted with siblings tend to be pre-adolescent and needing to be looked after for their own protection or during a family crisis. Adolescents - who more often come into care because of their own behaviour

- are seldom admitted with siblings (Farmer and Parker and Rowe et al 1989).

Earlier findings by Aldgate that children who came into care alone leaving brothers and sisters at home were destined for a long stay have been confirmed in recent studies, but definitions of 'sibling' may differ since half or step siblings may or may not be included.

There is also confirmation from research that children who are away from home, like being with siblings, but separation is a common experience. Whitaker et al (1985) found that children in residential placements with siblings 'almost always valued this and saw their sibling as a source of support and protection'. When separated, some accepted this casually but 'a significant number struggled with feelings of loss, frustration and bewilderment, sometimes years after the separation took place'. Most wanted to see their 'lost' siblings more often and some feared their siblings missed them.

Rowe et al (1984) found that long-term foster children placed with a sibling were usually glad about this and mentioned the benefit of having someone to talk to about their family of origin, while Fisher et al learned that children and young people who had been separated sometimes thought that this was a punishment.

Some groups of children were more prone to separation than others. Thus children of mixed parentage were more likely to be separated than were West Indians or Africans. Adolescents were more likely to be in separate placements while younger children were usually kept together. (It has not been clear whether the separated adolescents and their siblings had come into care at different times - and may indeed scarcely have known each other - or whether they had been split up while in care.) 'Child Care Now' reports that in only 14% of placements which ended where the child was under 11, were there siblings in care but not in the same placement. Foster homes and residential placements were similar in this respect. By contrast, in two-thirds of adolescents' residential placement endings the young person had at least one sibling who was placed elsewhere by the local authority. The same was true for half the adolescents' foster home endings.

Further evidence about separations comes from the SSI report 'Inspection of Community Homes' (1985) which says that there was little evidence of residential care being used to keep siblings together. And though in his study of children's homes Berridge found that 40% of the children and young people in his sample were with at least one sibling, he comments that many others had siblings in homes elsewhere. In Whitaker's study, 10 out of 34 children interviewed had siblings living somewhere else but 11 were placed with at least one sibling.

In their study of permanent placements, Wedge and Mantle found that social workers had a 'general assumption' that siblings should be placed together. Reasons for separating siblings were usually recorded, but reasons for placing them together were not. They also found that decisions about splitting or keeping together were not related to positive or negative relationships between siblings.

Both Wedge and Mantle and Farmer and Parker comment on the lack of information in records about sibling interaction. (Wedge and Mantle actually question whether adults are able to assess sibling ties because other research suggests that children modify their behaviour to siblings according to circumstances.) Farmer and Parker state: 'Little attention was paid to a child's relationships to household members other than the main parent figure; this was especially true of other children whether siblings or not.'

The pros and cons of keeping siblings together if their needs seem very different is inevitably a matter for anxious debate among practitioners and decision makers. Until recently, research provided little assistance, but some useful pointers are emerging from recent studies. Although the evidence is sometimes conflicting, the overall conclusion seems to be that being with a sibling usually has a helpful effect on stability.

1) **Placement at home.** In the Farmer and Parker study, returning 'home on trial' with a sibling was associated with successful outcomes.

2) **Long-term foster placements.** Berridge and Cleaver reported more breakdowns when the child had siblings in care but was separated from all of them (50% breakdown) than when placed with *all* siblings in care (33% breakdown) or with *some* siblings (26% breakdown). However, these

findings were not entirely supported by the outcomes data in 'Child Care Now'.

3) **Adoption and 'permanent' foster placements.**

i) In a survey of the outcomes of over a thousand 'special needs' adoption placements Thoburn and Rowe found that sibling placements break down *less* often. Only 18% of placements with one or more siblings broke down compared with 24% of single child placements. (This difference is statistically significant and still found when other variables are held constant.)

ii) After studying 'permanent' placements of siblings placed together or separately, Wedge and Mantle concluded that the impact can work both ways. Multiple placements may put too much stress on the new parents, but a child's adverse reaction to separation from siblings can also cause disruption. When siblings are placed together, the younger one may be more in jeopardy because of problems in the older one(s), but conversely, being placed with a younger sibling may reduce the chance of an older child feeling rejected by the new family.

iii) Intensive study of a small number of adoption placements of 9-10 year old boys left Rushton et al equally uncertain about the wisdom of splitting or separating sibling groups. They noted more progress in children placed with one or more siblings but point out that those placed alone tended to have more serious problems to start with.

c) 'Step-siblings' and other children

(The term 'step-sibling' is used for new members of reconstituted families and for established 'own' children in foster and adoptive families.)

The well-known risk of placing children into families where there are 'own' children close to them in age has been most strongly reinforced by Wedge and Mantle, by Berridge and Cleaver, and, to a lesser extent, by Fenyo et al (1989) in an examination of teenage placements.

In their study of sibling groups referred for permanent placement, Wedge and Mantle found that the presence of step-siblings who were less than three years older than the placed child was associated with sharply increased risk of disruption, but having much older step-siblings seemed to be helpful. Children under eight years old were the most affected by having step-siblings close in age. It seems to have mattered less to older children. Wedge identified three groups: (A) placements in which the new child was the youngest by at least three years; (B) placements with step-siblings where the age gap was less than three years; (C) placements with no step-siblings. There were no disruptions in group A, but in group B where there were step-siblings close in age, the disruption rate for younger children was very high and risk for the older children was also substantial as the table below makes clear.

Group	Age	No Disruption	Disruption	Total
Group A (Step-Sibs with at least 3 yr age gap)	Under 8 8 and over	14 (100%) 4 (100%)	— —	14 (100%) 4 (100%)
Group B (Step-Sibs with less than 3 yr age gap)	Under 8 8 and over	2 (20%) 11 (65%)	8 (80%) 6 (35%)	10 (100%) 17 (100%)
Group C (No Step-Sibs)	Under 8 8 and over	50 (88%) 24 (77%)	7 (12%) 7 (23%)	57 (100%) 31 (100%)

(From Wedge & Mantle 'Sibling Groups and Social Work')

Berridge and Cleaver discovered that no less than 48% of their sample of long-term foster children had been placed in a household in which there was a natural child within five years of age. They remark: 'As Trasler and Parker predicted 20 years ago, over 40% of such placements ended prematurely, compared with only 25% of those where no such child was present.'

Fenyo and his colleagues, studying a special teenage fostering scheme, found that the presence of other young people within two years of the age of the foster child was linked with breakdowns. They comment: 'the effect of the presence of teenagers of similar age increases with age and disproportionately so. The well known research result about similar aged children, stemming from the early breakdown studies and reinforced by later ones, would appear to apply with equal and probably greater force to the teenage foster care population. The implications for practice are obvious.'

Lack of detail in records made it impossible for Farmer and Parker to be so explicit about the effect of step-siblings on 'home on trial' outcomes, but they note that change among other children in the household to which a child returns is associated with less satisfactory outcomes even if the adults in the household remain the same.

The presence of other children can also be a problem for children and young people in residential care, but for different reasons.

During their observations and interviews in four children's homes, Whitaker and her colleagues learned much about the stress children experienced from their peers. They report:

> 'Thirty out of thirty-four children reported personally experiencing physical abuse, verbal tormenting, feelings of intense aggravation with particular children and/or alarm at witnessing aggressive exchanges between other children.' A good deal of bullying was observed, so: 'In order to survive among their peers, many children felt compelled to adopt a "tough" persona and an aggressive attitude . . . Some of the quieter children felt resentful that they were not protected enough by the residential workers, and did not have the back-up of staff in frightening situations. Observations showed that on the whole staff tended to leave the children to fight their own battles.

> 'There was little indication of strong, positive and mutual bonds between unrelated peers . . . Although one could observe many instances of amicable interaction and play, in general the peer group was far more likely to be a source of stress rather than a source of support.'

Colton's detailed exploration of daily life in residential care (1989) supports Whitaker's views. He found that young people in residential care tended to perceive their peers as rather unfriendly and aggressive and did not consider them as a positive influence.

4 The Main Findings on Promotion of the Child's Welfare and their Implications for Policy and Practice

1) Because of the deprivation and distress in the families from which children are admitted, it is likely that many of them will need a variety of remedial services including treatment for physical or sexual abuse.

2) The level of family discord and fragmentation which is reported indicates that practical services alone will often be insufficient and help with family relationships may be essential for effective preventive services.

3) The availability of functioning family and social networks seems to be a critical determinant of the need for admission and thus a necessary focus for preventive work.

4) Initiatives are needed to ensure that more attention is paid to the health needs of children being looked after by local authorities. The value of growth charts still needs to be emphasised and health care should be part of preparation for independence.

5) Recognition of the links between school achievement and both psychological adjustment and employment opportunities should lead to more emphasis on enabling children and young people to enjoy school and gain some qualifications while they are being looked after by local authorities. The need for continuity in education and the value of a sense of permanence emerge from research as important factors associated with school achievement and have obvious practice implications.

6) Research findings on the loneliness and day to day problems experienced by young care leavers calls into question the appropriateness of current practice which encourages ever earlier moves to 'independence'. They highlight the unwisdom of equating 'independence' for teenagers with managing alone and without regular support.

7) The provision of suitable accommodation is crucial for the welfare of those moving into independent living but building and maintaining support networks is also essential.

8) Fulfilling even the rather basic requirements of the 1989 Act in relation to care leavers will require a major effort to develop policy and practice guidelines, and to find the resources for urgently needed new programmes and accommodation.

9) Ethnic monitoring is an essential pre-requisite to the provision of services for black and minority ethnic children,

families and carers. It should be carried out routinely and translated into policy, service design and practice which should in turn be monitored.

10)   Special attention should be directed toward the situation of mixed parentage children who are at present in care in disproportionate numbers and at risk of multiple admissions to care or accommodation.

11)   The cultural backgrounds of children's families and the influence of this on their family relationships need to be better understood. Cultural issues should receive more attention both in the provision of services and in direct work with children and their families.

12)   Placement change continues to be a serious problem. The negative effects of breakdown are well known but the damage done by discontinuity of relationships due to administrative moves and staff changes deserves wider recognition. Every effort should be made to maintain and preserve friendships and affectionate relationships with the important people in each child's life.

13)   Nothing in recent research findings contradicts earlier messages about the problems of long-term care, the need for prevention and the difficulty any public body must have in acting as an effective parent. However, comparatively little is known about the damage and distress which some children suffer in their own homes and there is a risk of so denigrating the care system that virtually any alternative is considered acceptable. Short, medium and even lengthy periods in care or accommodation *can* be beneficial and may be the appropriate and least detrimental way to help particular children. Inflexible policies about admission or about the timing of 'permanency' plans can have detrimental effects and should be revised.

14)   The period after which children are likely to have a long stay in care has been found to be even shorter than previously thought - weeks not months. Policy, procedures and practice all need to take account of this and concentrate assessment and rehabilitative efforts immediately after admission instead of taking a 'wait and see' approach.

15)   Careful thought will be needed about how respite care can best be used to sustain families under stress. Some way will have to be found to enable children to return to the same placement if

they are going to have frequent or regular periods in accommodation. Unless the supply of respite care families is sufficient to permit this, some children are going to suffer a series of upsetting changes. There may be a role for small networks of carers all known to child and parents like an extended family. Some form of specialised residential provision - perhaps linked to the family carers - may also be appropriate. The research finding that socially disadvantaged families may find it difficult to use respite care, means that special consideration will have to be given to meeting their needs and feelings.

16) Agency policies and practice need to take seriously the now well established research finding that visiting is the key to discharge. Contact enhances the welfare of placed children and does not increase the risk of breakdown.

17) Concepts of permanence should be broadened to include the possibility of continued family contact through open adoption or permanent fostering.

18) Informal barriers to contact are widespread but may not be recognised. Agencies ought to examine not just their stated policies but the prevailing climate of opinion among their staff about birth parents and the maintenance of family contact. Staff may need more support and encouragement to do this work.

19) Premature or routine termination of contact when permanent placements are planned can do children a serious disservice by precluding the possibility of continued contact of some sort.

20) Relatives provide a placement resource which should always be considered. The stability of such placements - especially for long-term cases - makes it worth trying hard to seek out relatives and overcome obstacles.

21) Relatives are also an important source of family contact. Visits by grandparents or aunts and uncles can often be encouraged even if visiting by parents cannot be permitted.

22) More attention should be paid to the role of siblings and other children. The importance of child-to-child relationships has been insufficiently recognised. Changes in the child members of the family to which a child returns or the presence of 'own' children close in age to a foster child are both associated with

negative outcome, whereas placement with siblings is generally beneficial and sibling ties are valued by children.

23)   Other children and young people may be a source of stress rather than support and residential staff could be more alert to the need to protect children. Leaving them to fight their own battles is likely to be inappropriate.

Part Two Partnership with Parents and Carers

1 Background

Although the word 'partnership' does not actually appear in the Children Act 1989, the concept permeates all the sections in Part III which deal with services provided by local authorities for children and families. Instead of the terms 'parental rights and duties', the Act refers to 'parental responsibilities'. These encompass both duties and rights and may be shared but not extinguished except through adoption. The position of unmarried fathers is strengthened.

The Act clearly envisages services which are a support to families rather than taking over from them, and though the authorities' powers will still be great in relation to children on care orders, in other instances they will be considerably reduced. The greatest change will be in relation to children for whom 'accommodation' is provided. This replaces the status of voluntary care in earlier legislation and in these cases the authority will be accountable to the parents. This new relationship and change in the balance of power requires a radical shift in thinking on the part of both administrators and social workers. It will not be easy to achieve especially because, as Marsh (1990) has pointed out, social workers are likely to believe that they already try to work in partnership with parents.

Other changes introduced in the Act itself or in Regulations will help to reinforce the concept of partnership. Authorities will be required to:

- consult and inform parents;

- ascertain their wishes and feelings about placement plans;

- enter into written agreements;

- avoid compulsory measures as far as is consistent with meeting children's needs.

All of these changes can be linked with research studies reported on in 'Social Work Decisions in Child Care'. The most obvious link is the Act's emphasis on partnership rather than compulsion. The evidence from research was that taking compulsory powers not only failed to achieve better planning and security but was often counter-productive. Family ties were more difficult to maintain after court orders and relationships between parents and social workers were often damaged. Packman (1986) and the Dartington research team found parents distressed, disgruntled, even outraged by compulsion. Parents felt that they had no say in the decisions that had been made, that matters had been taken out of their hands and they were now unable to influence social workers' plans for their children.

While there is no doubt that these research findings on parents' experiences and attitudes influenced the legislation, the crucial question now is, can they assist the implementation of the new law and regulations? Can they help social workers to understand what needs to be changed and why? What aspects of good practice should be developed and extended?

If a partnership is to be established on a secure basis, there needs to be shared perceptions and agreement on what has gone wrong and on the more difficult area of what has to be done to improve matters. The researchers show how easy it is to be unaware of serious differences in perspective and to misinterpret actions and responses. During a recent study of child care and decision making in Northern Ireland, Kelly (1990) found that 'it was very difficult to find examples of social workers and parents . . . agreeing on the difficulties and working together to try and resolve them'. Some excerpts from 'Decision Making in Child Care' may further serve to illustrate the shaky foundation on which work with children and families is apt to rest:

> *'Often inadequate attention was paid to the history of the clients' problems, to issues of discipline and authority within the home, to parents' expectations of the workers' intervention and to establishing a knowledge base common to all participants. Too often, disagreements about the nature of problems and about methods of handling them remained unexplored undercurrents in exchanges between workers and clients . . . (This approach) was extremely unlikely to lead to substantial agreement over the **purpose** of care.'* (Fisher et al)

> *'It seems probable that social workers quite often misinterpret natural parents' behaviour at the time of admission because the psycho-social study of the family is not sufficiently thorough . . . We have some painfully vivid examples of cases where parents were considered rejecting or uncaring because*

the problems they were facing had not been properly understood.' (Rowe et al 1984)

'In relation to parents, workers constantly underrated the amount of continued responsibility and concern they felt for their children, tending to misinterpret relief as rejection.' (Fisher et al)

2 The Current Studies

Evidence from the current studies is that not much has changed and there is still a long way to go before partnership can be confidently expected.

The principal research findings are from the Dartington Research Unit's work on 'Access Disputes in Child Care' and Farmer and Parker's work on 'home on trial' placements, but there is also some useful evidence from enquiries about the use of written agreements and parents' attendance at reviews and case conferences.

A study of access disputes inevitably has to focus on a series of cases in which relationships between parents and social services departments are strained, and it is not at all surprising that parents whose access to their children has been officially terminated will frequently be hurt and angry and there will be little or no sense of partnership. Of much greater concern is the backcloth to these disputes, with parents feeling helpless against powerful bureaucracies and impersonal administrative processes while hard pressed social workers, seeking to give priority to the welfare of the child, find it easier and quicker to take control than negotiate and conciliate. The Dartington team concluded: ' . . . for many parents, the longer their child stays in care the more the role of the social worker as controller and arbiter seems to increase.'

Although terminations of access are hardly likely to be the result of joint planning between parents and social workers, one would expect a very different picture in relation to decisions to return children 'home on trial'. Yet Farmer and Parker found surprisingly little evidence of parental participation here either. Parents attended conferences or planning meetings in only 19% of 'disaffected' cases and a mere 12% of 'protected' cases. Written agreements were unusual and even where they had been used, the researchers found that 'there was rarely evidence that they specified exactly what was expected during the placement'. Thus there was no certainty that parents and social workers would have similar perceptions of what should be done or of shared planning.

Confirmation of these findings comes from a child care review carried out by Wiltshire Social Services (1990). Their report states that parents were in attendance in only 10 out of 30 conferences on rehabilitation and in summing up the findings over a range of cases it concludes that 'parents and children were rarely involved in decision making in a formal way and even their involvement in consultation was limited'. It goes on to say: 'The Children Act will lead to radical change in the working relationship between social workers and parents and children.'

A particularly disappointing finding of a survey of 352 family centres - where one might expect a very participatory style of work - was that less than a quarter had any parents on their management group. (Vallender 1990).

Although written agreements or 'contracts' have been part of the social work scene for some years, they have not been widely used in relation to children in care except in specialist foster care schemes. Pilot work done by the National Foster Care Association and Family Rights Group has given clear indications of the distance between a general welcome to the idea of using agreements and actually putting them into regular social work practice.

3 Barriers to Partnership

It seems certain that however welcome and necessary the principle may be, genuine partnership will be difficult to achieve for several reasons:

1) Tradition and bureaucracy.

2) The level of skill, sensitivity and time required from social workers.

3) The parents' personal problems and variable willingness to co-operate.

4) Problems over the balance of power.

The parents of children who need to be looked after by local authorities are almost always very disadvantaged people, many of whom also have serious personal problems. As research has repeatedly shown, their family relationships tend to be turbulent and fragmented; they may suffer from mental illness or have drug or alcohol problems. Their past experience of officialdom will probably have been stressful and they are likely to be at best ambivalent about accepting help with their children. In a few cases children have to be actively protected against their parents for the time being at least. None of these characteristics offers an easy basis for reciprocal trust between parents and social workers and the latter will need to take initiatives and work hard to build a genuine partnership.

In the conclusions to her study of short-term fostering, Stone comments: 'Many children seem to be the victims of conflict, both conflict within their families and between their family and outside agencies.' She questions whether the philosophy of 'partnership' proposed in the 1989 Children Act will be sufficient to minimise these areas of conflict, and suggests that more positive and active solutions should be found through counselling and conciliation services.

Two of the recent research reports highlight problems over the balance of power. In discussing their findings, Farmer and Parker reveal the difficult situation faced by social workers supervising 'home on trial' placements in which they carried responsibility and had authority but lacked power. Under current legislation, the only sanction available was the removal of the child. This is a step which social workers were extremely reluctant to take even if feasible - which, in the case of difficult older adolescents, it may not have been. (The new style supervision orders which will be brought in under sections 31, 35 and 36 of the Act may prove helpful in these situations.) These researchers considered that there were 'real questions about how the responsibilities of the authority could be adequately discharged when the social workers' leverage, or even access, was so problematic'.

In most social worker/parent relationships, however, the balance of power has been all the other way. In their report on access disputes, Millham et al build up a compelling picture of the imbalance of power between parents and social services departments in relation to decisions about access. Although most parents found the receiving of a termination of access notice deeply disturbing and nearly half decided to try and seek redress, very few actually obtained access orders through the courts. Even the few orders made in the juvenile court were likely to be overturned when the local authority appealed to the High Court. In spite of legal representation, parents are at a serious disadvantage in court because the authority has the information, the experience and the resources to obtain expert advice and opinion. This remains true even though the 1989 Act gives parents much stronger and clearer rights over contact and opportunities to get any grievances aired. Of course the studies could not take full account of the new role and influence of guardians *ad litem*. The 1989 Act will further reinforce the importance of their role in court cases.

Our long-standing traditions of child rescue have meant that first Children's departments and then Social Services departments have tended to marginalise parents even when acting benevolently toward them. The strong emphasis on the welfare of the child has often pushed parents' needs and wishes into the background and departments have assumed full control over children admitted to their care and assumed they knew best. With the benefit of hindsight, we can appreciate that there has been remarkably little sense of being responsible to parents. For instance, the research demonstrates that written information for parents and children is still conspicuous by its absence. It has not previously been required that departments should report regularly to parents on their children's progress and there may or may not have been any consultation over such matters as choice of school, permission to smoke or hair style and clothing.

It would be unwise to assume that changes in legislation can easily bring fundamental shifts in long established priorities and ways of dealing with people. 'Access Disputes in Child Care' offers salutary reminders of the difficulty of achieving changes of attitude in large organisations. The HASSASSA* legislation and Code of Practice on Access were shown through this research to have had a variable but limited effect on practice and outlook in local authorities. Few used them to take a fresh look at access arrangements for all parents and few either set up the complaints procedures recommended by the Code or involved elected members in access decisions.

A similar note is struck by Robbins (1990) in the SSI report of a review of child care policy statements. All English authorities were asked to send in documents on their complaints procedures. The report states: 'Overall the response from authorities is disappointing, both in quantity and in quality.' It seems that only a minority of social services departments have had an effective complaints procedure for parents or children.

Resistance to practice change is clearly widespread and must be anticipated during implementation of the Act. Writing about his current Partnership Research and Development Programme, Marsh (1990) comments on 'the belief that genuine commitment must somehow be automatically converted into action'. It is easy to be far too sanguine that what is accepted in theory as good practice, is actually being practised. Marsh has coined the phrase 'the DATA syndrome'. This phenomenon becomes evident when staff respond to suggestions about greater partnership with parents by saying, either implicitly or explicitly, 'we Do All This Already'.

---

*The Health and Social Services and Social Security Adjudications Act 1983

4 Some Encouraging Signs

Although partnership with parents will not be easy to develop, there are already encouraging signs that it can work and that good practice really does help.

Packman (1989) has summed up the research findings about the qualities in social workers which parents find most helpful. They are all qualities which fit naturally into a partnership approach and it is clear that this is an approach which parents will welcome:

> 'What appears to be valued most is the style of the intervention. Social workers are experienced as helpful if they really listen and take pains to understand the difficulties from the family's point of view. They are also valued if they are practical as well as sympathetic and supportive and do more than just listen. Honesty and directness are important qualities that parents are well able to appreciate - even if some messages are hard and unpalatable . . . workers who "act natural" and present a human rather than an official face are also much appreciated . . . Above all most parents wish to participate in decisions about their children and to be included as important partners in negotiations.'

Further support comes from two of the more recent research studies. Farmer and Parker found that social workers were effective in supporting 'home on trial' placements when they had a clear sense of purpose and, among many other things, involved parents in six-monthly reviews. Millham et al's research on access disputes showed that parents were less upset and had a better understanding of the otherwise daunting procedures for obtaining access orders when they had had more frequent contacts with social workers and had opportunities for internal hearings of their complaints about access.

But the most encouraging indications on partnership are the successes of respite care schemes. So far, formal respite care schemes have been largely confined to children with disabilities, though individual respite arrangements are made for a wide variety of children and young people including adolescents in 'professional' foster homes. One or two authorities have developed imaginative arrangements such as Hertfordshire's 'guesting' (emergency 'cooling off' placements for up to 72 hours without formal admission), Strathclyde's short stay refuge for older children, or Oxfordshire's relief care scheme. All these projects are based on principles of partnership and of concern for parents as well as children. It should be accepted and stated as a matter of policy that an opportunity for parents to attend to their own legitimate needs is an essential element of relief care.

British research on respite care is still in the basic, early stages of trying to determine what is going on, though some work by Aldgate and Webb will provide much needed information on the feasibility of using respite care as a preventive service. Concern has been expressed by Webb (1990) over the potential confusion from the 'ad hoc' use of the term respite. It is used to cover crisis, occasional and regular care and whether the stress for which relief is needed is caused by the child's disability or behaviour or by the parents' personal problems. He is also worried about the lack of a conceptual model on which new development could be based. Nevertheless Webb described respite as 'central to principles of partnership' and though it does not include the term, respite care is inherent in the Children Act's introduction of 'accommodation' as a service to children in need and families under stress.

5 Partnership with Carers

Relationships between field social workers and residential staff and between social workers and foster parents (or foster carers as they are now more generally known) are by no means always easy or harmonious. For several decades researchers have explored their differing perceptions, but in practice uncertainties remain about roles and relationships. One indication of foster carers' dissatisfaction is the setting up of independent services by groups of foster carers. Another is the continued high drop-out rate of newly recruited foster families.

The National Children's Bureau study of fostering in Warwickshire (Cliffe 1990) shows how putting additional resources into support services for foster carers enabled them to look after a much wider range of children and young people without experiencing an unusually high breakdown rate. Another potentially hopeful development is the increased use of written agreements required by the new regulations. This should clarify what the placement objectives are and who will be responsible for what aspects of carrying them out, thus minimising the risk of the confusion, disappointment and disillusion which can mar collaborative working relationships.

The severe behaviour problems shown by some foster children can be a source of tension in the relationship between social workers and foster carers. Social workers sometimes find it difficult to offer the practical advice which the carers are looking for (Keane 1983). Aldgate and Hawley (1986) offer an insight into the benefits of partnership in this area. They found that social workers may feel guilty about admitting their ignorance, but 'where ignorance had been shared, this enabled social workers and foster parents to identify together problem areas for which they needed to seek help from elsewhere'.

The style of work with adoptive parents which is likely to be most effective emerged clearly from a number of studies (Macaskill 1987, Yates 1985). Once again this proves to be based on partnership principles. Yates includes the following skills and attitudes as among those most appreciated:

1) Interest in and commitment to the new family along with reinforcement of the adopters' parental authority.

2) Warmth, ability to listen and a capacity to 'stand back' and then reflect back what is going on.

3)   Providing opportunities for problem sharing without reservation so that tensions can be released and a process of problem sharing engaged in.

A remarkably similar list emerged from Thoburn et al's detailed and longitudinal study of Children's Society placements in East Anglia (1986). They say:

'The parents wanted, and for the most part received, the sort of service which a social worker asks of a team leader. They accepted the workers' ultimate authority, but had confidence that the authority delegated to them as parents would not be interfered with unless this was necessary in the interest of the child. Reassurred by this, they wanted regular opportunities to describe their activities, explain their difficulties, explore their ideas for alternative ways of handling them, consider other suggestions and receive offers of help in any joint work to be done. They wanted to share their happy moments and successes, receive praise and share pleasure. For this to happen they needed to feel valued and for all members of the family to be cared about. Finally, they needed to know that in a crisis competent help would be speedily available to them.'

This seems a good example of partnership - and it is evidently successful because the Society's placements were remarkably stable and satisfactory in spite of the very serious problems which the children not only presented at placement but often continued to display. The message that comes from research on social workers' relationships with carers is that while partnership cannot offer a magic solution to entrenched problems, it does provide a solid base for effective work toward solving them.

That more attention should be given to the needs and feelings of carers' own children is a theme which comes through strongly from Thoburn's follow-up of older child adoptions (Thoburn 1990) and from an unpublished pilot study by von Arnim (1988) which looked at the effect on host children aged 8-12 whose parents fostered adolescents. Both of these studies showed that the natural children may gain a great deal from the adopted or fostered newcomer. But they can also pay a heavy price, especially at certain stages of their development. Their problems can also cause placement breakdown.

6 The Main Findings on Partnership and their Implications for Policy and Practice

1)   Research shows that partnership with parents has not been integral to past or current social work practice. Some fundamental changes in attitude will be required if the spirit of the new Act is to be fully implemented.

2)   Real partnership with parents or carers is based on a shared perception of what has gone wrong and what needs to be done. To establish this method, practitioners will need to develop their self-awareness and their capacity to empathise with parents' and carers' feelings and concerns.

3)   Written agreements are crucial for partnership work and required by Regulations. In the past, their use has been limited and patchy, so developing this skill should be a high priority for in-service training. It needs to be supported by policy and in procedure manuals.

4)   Attendance of parents at reviews, case conferences and planning meetings should become a normal part of policy and practice.

5)   Before departments and individual social workers will be able to accept the role of parents' agent when providing accommodation, there will have to be a radical re-think of past and future roles and expectations.

6)   The experience of the very limited effect of the Code of Practice on Access gives an indication of the problems of achieving change in long-established patterns of work. This is reinforced by the DATA (doing all this already) syndrome which inhibits learning and change.

7)   Relief care schemes offer a useful partnership model.

8)   A successful style of work with adoptive parents has now been identified and could profitably be emulated.

9)   The needs and feelings of carers' own children require closer attention.

PART THREE POLICIES, PLANNING AND DECISION MAKING

1 Background

A local authority's policy must, of course, be based on legislation and the profound changes required by the Children Act 1989 will inevitably lead to reconsideration and re-drafting of local authorities' child care policy documents. In the main, the Act deals with policy and planning issues indirectly. It assumes that policies will be drawn up to implement the legislation and that planning will take place in the context of these policies. New duties are laid down about ascertaining the extent of need and the provision of services for children and families. Special planning will clearly be needed in additon to the general duty to safeguard and provide for the welfare of each individual child which pre-supposes planning in order to achieve this. In relation to decision making, the Act is much more specific. In S22(4)&(5) it requires authorities to ascertain the wishes and feelings of the child, the parents and relevant others and to give due consideration to them. In particular, the authority must consider the child's religious persuasion, racial origin and cultural and linguistic background. More detailed instructions and recommendations are given in the Regulations and guidance documents which flow from the Act.

In the sections which follow, the research findings which relate to general policies and strategic planning are considered first, followed by those which concern plans and decisions for individual children. References are also made to two other Department of Health publications, 'A Sense of Direction: Planning in Social Work with Children' (HMSO 1989) and 'Child Care Policy: Putting It In Writing' (HMSO 1990). The former reviews Social Services Inspectorate reports and the latter reviews local authority child care policy statements.

2 Strategic Planning

a) The need for accurate information

The variety of children's ages, placements, legal status and lengths of stay makes the patterns of care very complex. It is all too easy to misinterpret statistics, to be unaware of local differences or to be misled by 'talk' rather than facts. However, if strategic planning is to be effective and if scarce resources are to be used efficiently, managers must have an accurate picture of local and national patterns of need and provision. Without reliable baselines, monitoring is impossible, deficits cannot be examined or costs predicted with any accuracy. The studies reported here provide a wealth of factual material on placement patterns and outcomes - some of it quite surprising.

Among the useful points emerging from research and discussed in the following paragraphs are: the misleading effect of static, year-end statistics; the continued importance of the residential sector; current use of foster and adoptive families; and links between age, aims and outcomes.

End of year figures, which have been the only national child care statistics available, do not reflect either the turnover of children in care or the number and types of placements which they experience. (A review of national data collecting is currently in progress.) Over a 12 month period, the six authorities covered in 'Child Care Now' made almost 5,000 new placements between them. This must have created a heavy workload. Wedge and Phelan confirm that in Essex the number of children experiencing care each year was 50% greater than the number in care at year's end, but this varied between different age groups. Planning for staff and placement resources needs to take account of this. It is also unwise to rely on annual statistics which show a steady decline in children in care but which mask the workload created by frequent admissions and discharges. The number of admissions to care has not declined nearly as sharply as the numbers in care at any one time as stays in care have been shorter particularly among younger children.

Many commentators, including the House of Commons Select Committee on Children in Care (1984), have thought that residential services were being reduced to the point of destruction. Research reports now disclose a different picture. Although the number of available places has declined dramatically, residential care is still widely used especially for adolescents. More recently, its potentiality for providing much needed specific and specialist services for particular children is increasingly recognised. So, too, is the importance of offering young people some choice about the type of placement they prefer.

The continued importance of the residential sector in the provision of a good child care service is emphasised by Berridge and by Millham et al. It is reinforced in Cliffe's study of residential and foster care in Warwickshire, which has been the only authority to close *all* its own residential establishments although it still makes some placements in facilities run by other agencies. Among its useful findings, this study showed that some young people experienced an unacceptably large number of unsuccessful foster placements when a suitable residential facility might have met their needs more appropriately.

The 'Child Care Now' study found that numbers of residential and foster placements were about equal each at 37% of the total. But whereas residential establishments (including hospitals and family centres) accounted for only 6% of pre-school placements, more than half of all placements of those aged 11+ were in some form of residential care. Conversely, foster homes accounted for 77% of placements of pre-school children, for 65% of placements of 5-10 year olds, but for only 15% of placements of young people of secondary school age. Even in authorities with special adolescent fostering schemes, foster placements of adolescents did not reach 25%. This not only highlights the importance of providing good quality residential services for teenagers, but also makes it clear that a major input of effort and resources is needed if foster family care for teenagers is to increase. (This was indeed the experience in Warwickshire.)

The information provided by 'Child Care Now' data points up the crucial importance of accurate information on trends and patterns and the very real danger of myths and misperceptions based on what is talked about and written about rather than what is actually happening. It is not only teenage foster placements that are far fewer in number than the interest in them would lead one to suppose. Adoptions of older children, too, are surprisingly infrequent given the amount of attention they receive. Over a two year period, the six authorities in 'Child Care Now' made only 40 placements of children aged five years or more where the aim was adoption. Nineteen of the 40 were made by one authority, so in the other five, older child adoption placements were extremely infrequent.

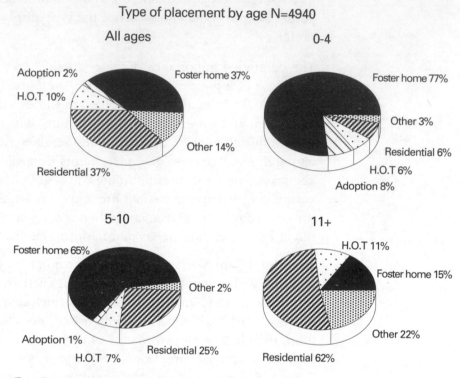

Type of placement by age N=4940

(From Rowe et al. 'Child Care Now')

A third topic where perceptions and reality differ is the aim and style of foster placements. This, too, has major implications for strategic planning. 'Child Care Now' shows that the bread and butter work of the foster care service is still the short-stay placement of young children during a family crisis or to give relief to hard-pressed parents (as encouraged by the new Act). The task-centred foster placements which receive the most attention in the literature account for only a third of all placements (though this rises to 43% of teenage placements). Since far more young children than adolescents are fostered, Rowe et al (1989) found that there were more task-centred placements of younger children. This must have implications for the selection, training and support of foster carers. For example, it is an unproductive use of scarce social work time to study and prepare applicants for traditional long-stay 'exclusive' placements if these are not needed. A brief foundation course is insufficient to equip people to play their proper part in task-centred placements. And to prepare carers but then leave them unsupported is a recipe for failure.

Without accurate data on the movement of children in and out of foster homes, there is also a danger that an authority might think that its foster care service is shrinking because its boarding out rate is going down. Rowe et al point out that:

'Well-developed preventive services, the use of residential family centres and emphasis on task focussed and time-limited foster placements instead of long-term fostering can all have the effect of lowering the boarding-out rate. The decline in long-term fostering means that as teenagers who are currently in long-term foster homes graduate out of the system, authorities are likely to find that their DHSS boarding-out rates dip noticeably, even if they are making a higher proportion of placements in foster homes than ever before.'

Accurate information on ages and placement aims can also help to prevent misunderstanding about placement outcomes. All the recent studies reinforce earlier research findings that the child's age is a crucial factor in determining the likelihood of the placement being successful. Breakdown rates rise inexorably with age at placement, so unless age is taken into account, comparisons of breakdown rates can be misleading. For example, while the evidence is that long-term foster placements are breaking down almost as frequently as 20 or 30 years ago, the children now being placed are much older. In reality, therefore, today's social workers are achieving a similar level of success with much more difficult placements. Success also needs to be measured by whether aims are met, and some aims are very much more difficult to achieve than others. 'Temporary care' can almost always be achieved, but 'assessment', 'treatment' or 'bridge to independence' are very much harder, and 'Child Care Now' reports the sobering finding that less than half of the placements of this type both met their aims *and* lasted as long as needed. It has to be recognised that as agencies seek to 'push out the frontiers', place older and more difficult children in families or set more complex aims, their breakdowns are bound to increase and aims will less often be fully met. Of course this does not mean that placements with an element of risk should not be attempted.

b) The need for better classification

Several recent studies highlight the importance of getting beyond 'global' categories and identifying specific groups of children or families and their needs. This is necessary for the development of policy, for planning resources and for providing appropriate regulations and guidance. The new vocabulary introduced by the Act provides a useful opportunity to re-think out-worn classifications.

Some of the long-established legal/administrative categories are shown by research to be positively unhelpful. A clear example is the group of children who are placed 'home on trial'. Farmer and Parker's detailed study shows up major differences between the children and young people who were on care orders for their own protection and the young people whose own troublesome behaviour brought them before the courts and subsequently into care. The researchers call them the 'protected' group and the 'disaffected' group respectively but consider that further sub-categories are needed. They say:

> '*We believe that there are important distinctions between, say, the fortunes of neglected and abused children when they go home on trial as well as differences in the way that social workers may have to approach the issues of their support and supervision. We also believe that it would be helpful to treat separately those who go home to parents from those who are placed with relatives and, especially, those who go to 'friends' since many of these friends are boyfriends or girlfriends of much the same age as the child in care. In short, we must not assume that home on trial placements form a homogeneous group: they do not.*'

Lumping all minority ethnic groups together as 'black' children also creates potential problems. It masks the serious over-representation of mixed parentage children and it makes it impossible to plan proper resources for fulfilling the Act's requirements to consider cultural, religious and linguistic needs. The umbrella term 'Asian' usually includes Ugandan Asians, Bangladeshis and Indians, and sometimes Malaysians, Indonesians and Singhalese. This fails to distinguish the very different backgrounds from which these children come. Asking questions about racial background has sometimes been a sensitive and controversial matter, but is easier in relation to the provision of services than for a national census. Enquiries about ethnicity will be essential in carrying out the duties laid down in Schedule 2 Part 1, which requires authorities to seek out and meet need.

Care-leavers form another administrative category which needs to be broken down into groups with differing needs. Leaving care schemes will need to be targeted on particular groups if they are to be effective, and young people in secure family settings usually do not want or need the same range of services as those struggling to live independently (Garnett).

Foster care and adoption also include such diversity of aim and type of placement that it is increasingly difficult to devise regulations and procedures that are appropriate for all. For example, Thoburn's research on permanent placements shows how the regular review and re-evaluation of aim which is essential in task-centred placements may undermine security in a 'permanent' foster placement. Planning and policies for recruitment, preparation and after-care of long-term and permanent placements will be more effective if the distinction between 'hard to place' and 'hard to bring up' is recognised.

The residential sector provides a final example of research pointing to the need for clearer classification. The range of establishments from observation and assessment centres to therapeutic communities, family centres, secure accommodation, family group homes and adolescent hostels is so wide that generalisations about relevance, effectiveness or scale of provision needed are likely to be either misleading or useless. Berridge's research in children's homes reveals a too frequent mis-match between the general aims of the establishment and the specific needs of the child or young person. Social Services Inspectorate reports also highlight problems arising from a lack of clearly stated objectives for each establishment leading to differing opinions among staff or between field and residential workers about the appropriateness of placements.

c) Local authority differences and structures

The Children Act, and the Regulations and guidance which flow from it, will of course apply to all local authorities and voluntary organisations. But as recent research studies make clear, there are still huge differences in the quantity, quality and style of the services provided in spite of a shared legal framework and broadly similar aims and problems. In an overview of the six authorities which made up their sample, the authors of 'Child Care Now' say: 'At times it was very hard to remember these

60

common threads as the differences always seemed to loom larger than the similarities.'

It is important that people who are responsible for the strategic planning of child care services should be aware of these differences and take full account of them. Geography, history, economics, politics and demographic patterns all impose or create major variations in need, resources and local expectations. Standards of practice should not vary, but methods may need to be adapted. What works well in one place may be far less effective elsewhere because of different attitudes, resources, structures and agency 'culture'. Unless people take account of these differences between authorities – and indeed between areas within one authority – some very misleading comparisons may be made and the wrong conclusions are easily drawn.

Among the many differences shown up by research, the following seem particularly relevant to planning and policy making:

1) **Admissions to care and accommodation**. Ever since the setting up of children's departments, there have been striking differences in rates of admission. Bebbington and Miles demonstrate that these continue. There are also differences in the characteristics of those admitted, and the reasons for and legal route of their entry. Some of these differences are demographic, e.g. the proportion of minority ethnic children. Others, such as age and legal status, are due to local policies or resources or to the operations of courts and/or police (e.g. the proportion of children who had been remanded varied from zero to 14%).

Bebbington and Miles conclude that the most important explanation for different reasons and rates of entry are the actual variations between areas in the circumstances of children generally, and they demonstrate the close association between deprivation and admission to care. A second reason identified by these researchers is that local authorities have developed different strategies for dealing with local need and may pay special attention to children with particular types of need or problem. Another root of differences is authorities' interpretation of the Children and Young Persons Act 1969 which will affect the legislative route by which children enter the care system. Changes introduced in the 1989 Act may require similar analysis.

2) Placement patterns. Patterns of placement reported in 'Child Care Now' show considerable variation from one authority to another and the researchers point out that children certainly do not have similar care experiences. Two of the six authorities in this study showed particularly striking differences in the way they were providing for their children. A primary school child in 'District' was four times as likely to have had a placement in a residential establishment as a child of the same age in care in 'Midshire'. As great or even greater contrasts were found in 'home on trial' placements for pre-schoolers - 2% in 'District' and 14% in 'Midshire' - and in use of observation and assessment centres for adolescents - 26% of teenage placements in 'District' and only 3% in 'Midshire'. Lodgings were used for 13% of teenagers in 'Midshire' but only 2% in 'District'. Similar though less extreme differences were found between the other authorities.

Other researchers, examining specific types of placement, report equally varied patterns, especially 'home on trial' (Farmer and Parker) and teenage fostering (Lowe 1990, Shaw and Hipgrave 1989).

3) Financial help for care leavers. Both Garnett and Bonnerjea mention huge differences in the average size of leaving care grants. Bonnerjea reports a range from £150 to £1,100 and Garnett found that the proportion receiving 'setting up home' monies varied from 29% to 60%.

4) Termination of access (contact). In their study 'Access Disputes in Child Care' Millham et al found considerable variation between authorities in the rates at which termination of access notices were issued, and these differences were not related to the characteristics of children in their care. However, they found an inverse relationship between 'de jure' formal terminations and the 'de facto' situations in which informal barriers led to withering of contact. The use of one method appears to cancel out the other.

Alongside these major differences in local authority policy and practice is the variety in social services' organisational structures. These have been at the centre of so much professional debate and are both the cause and the outcome of the saga of repeated 're-organisations'. Several research reports - in particular 'Child Care Now' and 'Access Disputes' - consider these variations and comment on the effect of various models. Their important, even if unwelcome, conclusion is that all organisational structures contain some problems and re-organisation may be a costly way of exchanging one set of difficulties for another. In an article on the pros and cons of specialisation for fostering staff which was based on 'Child Care Now' data, Hundleby (1989) says bluntly: 'It is mistaken to think that a re-organisation will deal with difficulties over practice or policy.' She goes on to say: 'Each of our project authorities gave credence to the view that what works in one department will not necessarily work in another, and that every organisational type has strengths as well as weaknesses.' Planners and managers need to be more aware that standards of practice depend much more on knowledge, skills, morale, pressures and resources than organisational patterns. Or, to put it another way, process issues are not cured by structural change.

d) Getting policy, guidance documents and research findings down to the practitioners

One of the problems identified in 'Social Work Decisions in Child Care' was that policies appeared to have only a limited effect on practice. Policies - as distinct from procedures - appear to be little known by field social workers. Packman paid considerable attention to trying to determine their effectiveness but found them hard to define:

'Looking from the top downwards in our sample departments, official policy statements were generally fragmented, partial and sometimes elusive and of uncertain status . . . Looking from the bottom up, the sense of confusion and ambiguity is intensified. In the social workers' eyes policy is not always acknowledged or recognised and its links with practice on a case by case basis are frequently obscure.' (Packman)

'Except when stated in the broadest and most abstract terms, child care policies do not command a consensus of support.' (Packman)

'Despite the excellence of the non-accidental injury handbooks, we found that in many social work offices copies were not available.' (Hilgendorf)

Sadly, recent reports echo much the same themes. In her review of policy statements, Robbins (1990) says:

'The kind of policy statements which were sent in are not the appropriate context for detailed practice guidelines. Nevertheless, it is important to ask whether all the aspects of policy which would help to ensure that a belief in planning is reflected in day to day social work are present . . . Only a minority of the documents included all these elements.'

Millham et al (1989) looked in detail at the way the DHSS Code of Practice on Access had been distributed and used in the departments they studied. They found that in departments with devolved or federal style structures, translations of the recommendations of the Code into practice were generally poor and distribution of the document was unsatisfactory. Although most team leaders received a copy, little information filtered down to those working directly with clients. The centrally organised authorities did noticeably better in this respect but overall the potential value of the Code was not appreciated. They conclude that the more that power is devolved to area teams, the greater the risks of confusion over policy or the intentions of legislation, although devolution may have other benefits.

The Wiltshire study disclosed extensive confusion among social workers about departmental policy. A typical comment (this time on rehabilitation) was: 'Existence of county policy is disputed. Fifteen respondents think there is one; fourteen do not and nine do not know.' Among the many questions posed by Wiltshire's praiseworthy self-examination of its child care practice was one on the use made of research and social work theory in the formulation of plans and decisions about children. They found that in many cases social workers seemed unaware of the existence of a body of knowledge which could assist them. The Social Services Inspectorate's report on child protection services in Rochdale (1990) commented that a surprising number of social workers dealing with long-term child protection cases had not read the Department of Health's guide 'Protecting Children'. Others admitted making little use of their department's written policies and procedures, preferring to rely on their senior social workers for advice. The problem was that seniors might not always be up to date.

3 Planning and Decision Making for Individual Children

a) The need for continued emphasis

Research findings indicate that considerable progress has been made in establishing the importance of planning for children and some success achieved in putting it into practice, although disturbing instances of lack of plans are also mentioned in a number of the SSI and other reports. 'Child Care Now' found little evidence of placements drifting on too long, and though Farmer and Parker found a worrying 27% of cases of 'protected' children where no plan had been made six months after admission to care, their sample included children admitted a number of years ago. They were able to demonstrate that well planned returns 'home on trial' were more likely to be successful and that child abuse procedures have led to more planning.

The problem now seems to be that of the quality rather than the quantity of planning. Sometimes rigid policies on 'permanence' lead to rigid and unnecessarily painful confrontational plans for particular children. Farmer and Parker found that case files lacked evidence of attention to details about what changes would be needed before a child could go home. The resulting lack of goals could lead to prolonged stays in care with 'home on trial' placements finally arranged because of pressure from child or family or because other placements had broken down. They say: 'Greater specificity about what is required to restore children home, joint agreement with parent figures about the assignment of tasks and commitment to a time scale would be beneficial'. This comment was made particularly about 'protected' children, but there was also little evidence of specific conditions or even recorded expectations for the 'home on trial' placement of 'disaffected' adolescents. The researchers concluded that this lack added to social workers' difficulties in exerting any control over the placements though they were fully aware of the immense problems of providing suitable services for badly behaved adolescents.

The need to set objectives is also highlighted by Whitaker et al. They point out that one cannot assess 'success' without knowing what the aims were. They found that aims and objectives for children in the homes they studied were stated in different ways and at different levels by different people. From this, the researchers developed certain views, e.g.:

1) Aims need to be specified with care and in detail.

2) It is useful to think of different categories and levels of aim: overall and instrumental aims; long term and short-term aims; aims related to helping the child to cope with life within the Home; aims related to helping a child make sense of his or her current and past life; and so on.

3) A hope is not an aim, or, as others have said, 'one cannot make an "is" out of an "ought".'

These researchers also make a number of recommendations. They urge that in addition to longer-term goals (e.g. fostering), short-term and situation-specific goals could be identified and worked on to the child's benefit. They suggest that: 'Certain aims, especially physical care and protection, can be stated as aims for all children in care. However, these can best be regarded as baseline aims. Beyond this, aims need to be thought out for specific children with their specific circumstances firmly in mind.'

b) Weighing up risks when planning placements

Planning for an individual child always involves weighing up the pros and cons of the various possible alternatives. Often, genuine effort to meet needs means taking a calulated risk. Research can never produce an exact answer about the degree of risk of a particular placement for an individual child because the interplay of the factors which determine success or failure will be unique in each case. However, research findings do offer a framework for informed decisions because they can provide information about general patterns of outcome. When research demonstrates that certain factors tend to be associated with the desired outcome - or the reverse - practitioners can take steps to maximise the positive factors and minimise risk by providing counterbalances to the negative ones.

Measuring outcomes is fraught with problems. At what stage, by what yardstick and in whose opinion are the outcomes to be assessed? Researchers are increasingly emphasising the complexity of these judgements and the inadequacy of the traditional equation of 'placement lasting' with 'placement success'. Farmer and Parker's evaluation of 'home on trial' placements found that some younger children's placements lasted but were detrimental (child neglected or abused), whereas some adolescents' placements broke down (often because of offending) but had been a positive experience. The same pattern is reported in studies of foster care and adoption. A placement may fail to last but have done good, or continue for many years but have been an unhappy experience.

Looking at permanent placements Thoburn reinforces the danger of over-simplification. She says: 'It is not enough to establish that the youngster remained in placement if it is not clear that "permanence" in any particular case has indeed contributed to "well-being".'

After investigating the various ways in which children, parents, residential staff and field workers looked at placement objectives and outcomes, Whitaker et al considered the problems of assessing whether aims are met when trying to define success. They concluded: 'Rather than think in terms of "success", it is better and nearer to the realities, to think in terms of a pattern of gains and losses or costs and benefits.'

In spite of these very important caveats, decision makers do need to have detailed and accurate data on breakdown rates since breakdowns are always undesirable and all too often damaging. The picture from recent research is as follows:

1) Placement at home

In their study of 'home on trial', Farmer and Parker report that 49% of 'disaffected' (mainly teenage) placements broke down, compared with only 38% of the 'protected' (mainly younger) group. About half the 'home on trial' placements in 'Child Care Now' also failed to last as needed. In this sample, the 5-10 year olds had slightly higher rates of premature endings than the older or younger age groups, but adolescents' placements were less often said to have met the placement aims. As a result, they were less often 'successful' according to that study's criteria.

Much more encouraging findings emerge from a report from the Barnardo's New Families project in Colchester (Trent 1989). Out of 244 children referred for adoption, 36 (14%) were restored home. Only a quarter of these placements broke down even though all these families had originally been judged as unable to bring up their children. It seems almost certain that this level of success was due to the very high level of social work offered.

The New Families staff used with these families and children the techniques of assessment, preparation and support which they had developed in their work on adoption placements. They had adequate time and specialist skills.

2) Foster family care

To make any sense, breakdown rates for different kinds of fostering need to be considered separately.

Short-term fostering. Definitions of 'short-term' may vary, but studies by Berridge and Cleaver and Russell et al (1988) show that about 20% of short-term foster family placements did not last according to plan.

'Professional' foster care for adolescents. Fenyo et al report a breakdown rate of 38%, and in 'Child Care Now' 53% of these placements did not last as long as needed.

Long-term fostering. In the three agencies in Berridge and Cleaver's sample, breakdowns within five years varied from 20% to 41%. The 'Child Care Now' survey found that 27% of the long-term foster placements made in the first year had broken down by the end of the second year. At first sight, it looks as if breakdown rates have not improved since the pioneer studies by Trasler, Parker and George in the 1960s. But as mentioned earlier, the children and young people now being placed in long-term foster homes are mainly of school age and include a number of teenagers, whereas 20 years ago most placements were of very young children.

Foster placements with relatives. Although foster placements with relatives have their own particular risks, recent research shows them to be the most stable of all placements. Berridge and Cleaver report no breakdowns while 'Child Care Now' found that relatives were taking older children with more complex problems and were doing better with them.

3) Adoption and permanent fostering

Traditional adoption placements of infants and very young children very seldom break down even though the eventual outcome may not always be a happy one. The average

68

disruption rate for those aged three or over at placement is around 20%, but it increases with age at placement, with a rapid rise from about the age of eight, (O'Hara 1988, Thoburn and Rowe, 1988). Comparisons between studies are complicated because many American studies include a high proportion of children adopted by their foster parents and British placements often include a rather unclear category of 'fostered with a view to adoption' which may mean 'adoption definitely planned' or may mean 'adoption perhaps if things work out well'.

Permanent fostering (i.e. placements clearly intended to be permanent rather than open-ended long-term) is a relatively new development and is used mainly for older children. Work by Fratter et al (1991) is showing that when age is taken into account, permanent fostering placements do not break down more often than adoptions.

4) Residential care

There are no breakdown rates as such because unplanned residential endings are usually classed as 'transfers'. In 'Child Care Now' 21% of residential placements were said not to have lasted as long as needed but only 16% were 'unsuccessful' in that they neither lasted nor met their aims.

5) Factors associated with breakdown

There is a very complex inter-relationship of factors which are associated with placement breakdown, and it really is important that those who read research reports realise that when a factor is found to be associated with a particular outcome, this does not mean that it caused this outcome. Simple cause-and-effect relationships are rare.

Nevertheless, when individuals or groups are making placement decisions and weighing up risks, it is necessary to bear in mind that in a number of studies the following factors have been shown to be associated with unsuccessful placements and a higher than average risk of breakdown:

● Age: breakdowns of all types of placement increase inexorably and often dramatically with increasing age at placement;

- Longer periods in care and/or on placement waiting lists;

- Previous placement breakdown;

- (For own family placements) previous unsuccessful attempts at return home;

- Other children in household close in age to the placed child (excluding siblings being placed together);

- The child or young person is ambivalent or opposed to the placement;

- The parents or caregivers have unrealistic expectations for this child.

- Severe behaviour problems;

- The child is cut off from all that is familiar by a combination of loss of contact with birth parents, siblings, relatives and friends; being placed alone; changing schools and neighbourhoods.

c) The basis for decisions

Scattered through recent research reports are strong indications that impressions, assumptions and personal or social values too often take the place of systematic observation or confirmed facts. Nor are the facts always set in an appropriate context.

The importance of making specific plans to meet the particular needs of individual children is linked with emphasis on the value of seeing the child and family in the context of their life history. As Farmer and Parker say: 'Decisions must be placed . . . in a context that has an historical dimension. It ought to go without saying that evidence of what has happened in the past provides an important insight into what will happen in the future.' Unfortunately, the Inspectorate's investigation into assessment and monitoring of abused children who have returned home (SSI 1986) found some social workers reluctant to recognise that background history is significant.

Although the Inspectors report on some excellent work, they found only three out of nine authorities where decisions were not only based on adequate assessment but also thoroughly considered and well recorded. They comment that elsewhere the picture was gloomy and records in a very poor state.

Whitaker et al's study of children's experience of residential care contains findings on adult perceptions about children's primary concerns which provide much food for thought about how well residential and field social workers really know the children for whom they are planning. The researchers found that the children's main concerns were:

- their family and home;

- their own outbursts of anger and aggression;

- the reasons for their being in care;

- their future.

Staff were not always aware of these preoccupations which did not fit too well with their adult assumptions about children's behaviour and reactions. In particular they were not tuned in to the 'serious and substantial concern about their upset or angry feelings and their expression of these in aggressive behaviour or temper tantrums' which were demonstrated by more than a quarter of the children. Staff assumptions were that on the whole children adapt easily and fairly quickly to changes in their circumstances and that unacceptable behaviour requires control and discipline through sanctions.

The conclusion reached by the researchers was that staff attitudes 'reflected those in the general culture, somewhat modified in those who had received professional training.' They list a number of consequences of these assumptions as they were applied to individual children. These included the following:

'a. *Several children had been separated from siblings on the grounds that one was a bad influence on the other or that they quarrelled a lot, and suffered in consequence.*

b. *Several children were labelled as bad and this, together with a failure to see that the badness was an understandable response to family stresses and/or was instigated or intensified by within-the-Home dynamics, led to unacceptable behaviour becoming an established pattern, punishments escalating; or the child being transferred.*

c. *Some children suffered the consequences of bullying, either directly as victims or through witnessing disturbing events. In consequence of the assumption that children should settle their own quarrels, they might be left to deal with such episodes themselves.*

d. *A number of instances were observed in which forthcoming changes were announced to the children abruptly and without adequate preparation. The researchers considered that this occurred because of the assumption of children's easy adaptability.'*

Similar concerns about the basis for decisions or planning are raised in relation to placements at home of children in care. Decisions made about 'home on trial' placements were questioned in the Wiltshire study. The report says that out of 29 questionnaires there were '23 different responses, many of which did not appear to be research or theoretical findings, but rather personal values or social work lore'.

Farmer and Parker found that one in four of the 'protected' children 'home on trial' was neglected or re-abused. They conclude that 'Further abuse and neglect might be tolerated if the social worker believed that the family was generally co-operative. Poor attendance at school was also very likely to be allowed . . . Reluctance to remove children in the first place is exceeded by the reluctance to remove them once they have been returned home on placement.' Their study showed that social workers have considerable ability to predict that problems may occur and their concerns about returning children home were usually justified and should be taken seriously. Nevertheless, it seems that local authorities have used different standards for 'home on trial' than for other placements and have tolerated conditions for children which others in the community would condemn. Success or failure of these placements may be 'defined in organisational terms and not take into account the poor quality of relationships that some children experience during "home on trial" placements.'

A recent exploratory study by Higginson (1990) in which 40 child protection conferences were analysed produced some serious, even shocking, findings about the basis on which child care decisions may be made. They call in question some of the fundamental assumptions about professional practice on which legislation and guidance must rest. Her comments apply to all professional people attending the conferences, not just the social workers, and they can apply to all group decisions not just conferences on abuse. They also reaffirm points made in a study of inquiry reports (DHSS 1982) which pointed out the common psychological reactions of denial in face of painful and unwelcome evidence and the dangers of misconstruing situations by reacting subjectively.

After finding that 'in half the cases, the level of professional concern was at variance with the evidence presented', Higginson carried out an in-depth analysis. She says:

'What I found was marked distortion of evidence: evidence was ignored, conclusions drawn beyond the evidence presented; potentially negative information consistently presented positively and vice versa. Unsubstantiated allegations went unchallenged, moral judgements were made, professionals contradicted their own evidence and silenced one another.'

'The professionals were concerned, experienced and intelligent yet the magnitude of the perceptual distortions indicated that a major force was interfering with their professional judgements.'

'Parents were judged to be dangerous according to whether they were thought to have wilfully transgressed community values. This led to perceptual distortions and evidence was interpreted to support stereotypic views of parental behaviour . . .'

It is tempting to dismiss these allegations as the bias of a particular researcher who has come to hasty and ill-considered conclusions on the basis of her preliminary findings. It has to be accepted that subjectivity is a perennial problem for both groups and individuals. However, corroborative evidence from other recent studies and the SSI investigations indicates that there is indeed serious cause for concern.

Clearly, there are genuine difficulties over interpreting evidence, and there are also problems over collecting and recording factual evidence on which sound decisions can be based and, if necessary, justified. The SSI reports, like most research studies, deplore the level of recording and express deep concern about the lack of basic information. Management may need to give some priority to improving and simplifying recording systems. It is easy to understand how social workers who feel overloaded and stressed may allow their recording to slip and never find time to organise files. Yet inevitably this risks setting up a vicious circle, with time wasted hunting for information or decisions made on less than adequate evidence. As a result outcomes are likely to be less positive than hoped and if plans are not written down, they can never be monitored. In addition to the potential damage to children and families, the result of decision making and planning on inadequate evidence or false assumptions is increased work, greater stress and less job satisfaction.

4 The Main Findings on Policies, Planning and Decision Making and their Implications for Policy and Practice

1)   There is an urgent need for improved national and local child care statistics which would give details on the turnover of children and their care careers, provide a basis for monitoring changes and developments and reduce the risk of misperceptions about what is going on. It will be most important that authorities co-operate fully with the Department of Health's plans to introduce new annual statistical returns.

2)   Managers should be aware that the fall in numbers in care shown in past annual statistics masks the workload caused by more frequent admissions, discharges and placement changes. The number of placements each year is usually double the number of admissions. The overall fall in numbers has also masked the fact that many young children are still being admitted for short periods.

3) Since residential care clearly continues to fulfil important functions in most departments, it is important to ensure that this resource is properly adapted to current use and that the aims and facilities of each establishment are appropriately matched to the young people's needs.

4)   Short-term placement of young children is still the major part of fostering services and deserves more attention than it receives. If the number of teenage placements is to be substantially increased, there will have to be a major input of resources to recruit and support more foster carers. Adequate preparation and support of carers is essential if placements are to succeed.

5)   Task-centred placements of young children are more numerous than such placements of adolescents. This has implications for recruitment, training and support of foster carers.

6)   Some of the categories which have been used to classify children or types of placement are too general and can be misleading. The changes which will flow from implementation of the Act and Regulations provide opportunities to develop improved classifications. Clearer differentiation of groups would help toward appropriate allocation of resources and social work effort. It is particularly important that racial and cultural differences are identified.

7)   Recognition of the wide differences between local authorities enables policy makers and managers to question their own priorities and placement patterns.

8)   Unless the differences between authorities' admission and placement patterns are understood, false conclusions can be drawn from comparisons of boarding out rates, breakdown rates, etc.

9)   Studies of various departmental structures have reinforced the message that re-organisation may solve some problems but usually creates others and there is no blue-print suitable for all types of authority. Improvements in practice are not likely to result from further organisational changes.

10)   Urgent attention must be given to how policies, directives and guidance can be got into the hands and minds of practitioners. This issue is critical in face of the evidence that staff are too often confused or unaware of policies and regulations, and the harsh reality that every child care document in every department will have to be adapted to the new legislation. If the channels of communication do not flow freely, the potentialities for misunderstanding and mistakes are extremely serious.

11)   Continued emphasis is needed on the importance of planning for individual children. The aggregation of these individual needs into departmental policies is another important issue.

12)   Good planning requires specifying in writing what needs to be done, by whom, how and within what time span. General aims about providing a good standard of child care are insufficient. Long and short-term goals need to be agreed for each child and young person if planning is to be effective and there should always be a contingency plan at least to cover short-term crises.

13)   Everyone involved in making placement decisions should be familiar with the research evidence on outcomes. Placement panels should list the risks and the counterbalancing factors and explain the reason for any placement which is made in spite of the presence of factors known to be associated with high risk of breakdown, e.g. an 'own' child close in age to a young child being placed in a foster or adoptive home, or placement at home when the family composition has changed during the child's absence.

14)   Better decisions would result from giving more attention to the past history of child and family.

15)   Much more weight ought to be given to detailed observation and carefully collected evidence. Generalised statements and unfounded assumptions must be challenged. The consequences of relying on personal values, making false assumptions or ignoring or distorting evidence can be very serious indeed. The implications of the research findings on current decision making are that all the professionals involved in child care decisions would benefit from some rigorous training in the collection and use of evidence and should be challenged to examine the values on which their views are based.

Part Four Conclusions

The preceding sections have shown that recent research reports have much to offer to managers and practitioners who face the exciting, if daunting, task of implementing the Children Act and initiating the major changes that will be required. Useful facts, explanations and ideas flow from the research findings and provide many suggestions for practice and policy developments. There is encouragement in the findings about progress already made, but the studies reported here demonstrate once again the complexity and difficulty of providing a good child care service. As the Act itself makes plain, it is no longer enough to look narrowly at the needs of an individual child, for the child's welfare has to be understood in the context of a web of relationships. It is not enough to offer a service. The way in which it is offered and the attitudes of the service providers are also crucial. Key concepts in the Act such as partnership or family contact are all underpinned and reinforced by evidence from research.

The cumulative effect of studying a large number of research reports is to become aware that certain issues are much more important than would be apparent from the amount of attention given to them in any one report. The full significance of a particular finding may not even be evident to the individual researcher because it is only when a series of studies comes together that these underlying issues can be perceived.

In spite of the variety of style and scope of recent studies, there is a recurrent theme which not only links them but comes through quite distinctly as being of profound importance. It is the whole question of evidence - how to gather, test, record and weigh it.

Social workers tend to think of evidence in terms of court hearings and reports, but evidence in the sense of 'facts which lead to conclusions' must be at the heart of every decision. The whole child care service, from strategic planning to monitoring of individual outcomes, is permeated by questions of evidence. Gathering, testing, recording and weighing evidence are tasks basic to professional competence, but are seldom addressed in these terms. The emphasis on relationships has tended to lead social workers to say 'I feel that . . . ' rather than 'I observed that . . . '. Failure to obtain, handle and interpret evidence appears to be a crucial factor in many of the continuing problems and deficiencies disclosed by the research findings even when the reports themselves do not refer to it explicitly.

Without adequate evidence about existing need and resources, strategic planning is a waste of time. Sound assessment of the problems and strengths of individual children and families must be based on clear, sufficient and well recorded evidence about past and present functioning. Decisions can only be as good as the evidence on which they are based, and if evidence is distorted, ignored or not weighed up carefully, the decisions will be flawed. They may even be dangerous if risks and benefits are not analysed and balanced objectively.

In relation to the marshalling and handling of evidence, strong similarities can be seen between the skills and attitudes required of researchers and those needed by social workers, even though social workers have a much more complex task, often work under much greater pressure, and need a wider range of skills. Both disciplines require: discerning observation and patient enquiry; accurate recording of findings; organisation of the information obtained; careful analysis; and, finally, the weighing up of evidence so produced. Both also demand persistence in obtaining the necessary data and testing it for reliability; attention to detail and accuracy; the separation of facts from opinions; objectivity; and an ability to set the evidence in context. What is markedly different is the amount of emphasis which social workers and researchers put on these aspects of their work.

Researchers are constantly challenging themselves and each other to get accurate complete data, to avoid bias, assumptions and the drawing of unwarranted conclusions. A social worker's role as service provider and/or therapist has inevitably meant that more emphasis has been given to empathy, negotiation and building relationships and less to objectivity and a rigorous search for reliable evidence. Social work is more than a science, but perhaps the most important message from recent research is that if progress is to be made in developing professional standards in the care of children, then more attention must be given to scientific disciplines in dealing with evidence.

Because of the importance of this issue, the final section of this document provides a series of 'tools for practice' or 'exercises' which should help to support and strengthen skills in this area. They are grouped under the heading 'Where is your evidence?'

References

ALDGATE, J, 'Foster children at school: success or failure', *Adoption and Fostering*, Vol. 14, No. 4, 1990. A memorial lecture drawing on the author's current research and discussing implications for practice and policy.

ALDGATE, J (ed.), *Using Written Agreements with Children and Families*, Family Rights Group, October 1990. A collection of papers given at a training day.

ALDGATE, J, PRATT, R & DUGGAN, J, 'Using care away from home to prevent family breakdown', *Adoption & Fostering*, Vol. 13, No. 2, 1989. A report of experience in one local authority.

ALDGATE, J & HAWLEY, D, *Recollections of Disruption*, NFCA, 1986. A detailed study of a small number of foster care breakdowns. Interviews with social workers and foster parents.

BAMFORD, F N & WOLKIND, S N, *The Physical and Mental Health of Children in Care: Research Needs*, ESRC, 1988. Two discussion papers.

BARN, R, 'Black children in local authority care: admission patterns', *New Community*, 16(2), January 1990. A cohort study of all children in the care of one London authority. Includes more intensive study with interviews of a sub-group of 80 cases.

BEBBINGTON, A & MILES, J, 'The Background of Children who enter Local Authority Care', *The British Journal of Social Work*, Vol. 19, No. 5, October 1989. Research conducted for the Department of Health in 13 local authorities.

BERRIDGE, D, *Children's Homes*, Blackwell, 1985. A detailed study of 20 residential establishments and the children living in them.

BERRIDGE, D & CLEAVER, H, *Foster Home Breakdown*, Blackwell, 1987. An extensive and intensive study of long-term, short-term and intermediate length fostering breakdowns in three agencies. Data from records of 372 cases and interviews with all participants in 10 cases.

BONNERJEA, L, *Leaving Care in London*, London Boroughs Children's Regional Planning Committee, March 1990. Information obtained from lengthy questionnaires completed by London boroughs and interviews with staff and young people in leaving care schemes.

CLIFFE, D, *An End to Residential Child Care? The Warwickshire Direction*, National Children's Bureau, October 1990. A detailed follow-up for 15 months of 215 child care cases excluding under 5s. Questionnaires completed by social workers.

COLTON, M, 'Foster and Residential Children's Perceptions of Their Social Environments', *The British Journal of Social Work*, Vol. 19, No. 3, June 1989. Paper reporting on some findings from a comparative study of 12 specialist foster homes for adolescents and 8 residential units.

DES, *Community Homes with Education*, HMI Series: Matters for Discussion 10, HMSO, 1980. A critical review of the education provided in community homes.

DHSS, *A Study of Inquiry Reports*, HMSO, 1982. An analysis of commentary on child abuse inquiries held between 1973 and 1981.

DHSS, *Social Work Decisions in Child Care: Recent Research Findings and their Implications*, HMSO, 1985. A discussion paper with research summaries.

DH, *An Introduction to the Children Act 1989*, HMSO, 1989. A detailed discussion/guide for social workers and other non-legally qualified staff.

DH, *The Care of Children: Principles and Practice in Regulations and Guidance*, HMSO, 1989. A statement of accepted 'best practice'.

DUNN, J, 'Sibling influences on childhood development', *Journal of Child Psychology and Psychiatry*, Vol. 29, No. 2, March 1988. A summary of existing knowledge from research.

FANSHEL, D & SHINN, E B, *Children in Foster Care - A Longitudinal Study*, Columbia University Press, 1978. A study of children in care in New York. Records, interviews with social workers and psychological assessments of children.

FARMER, E & PARKER, R, *Trials and Tribulations: Returning Children from Care to Their Families*, HMSO, 1991 (forthcoming). A major study of the practice and policy issues concerning 'home on trial' placements. Based mainly on case records.

FENYO, A, KNAPP, M & BAINES, B, *Foster Care Breakdown: A Study of a Special Teenager Fostering Scheme*, Discussion Paper

616, Personal Social Services Research Unit, University of Kent at Canterbury, January 1989. Examination of breakdowns and the possibility of prediction using logit analysis.

FISHER, M, MARSH, P & PHILLIPS, D with SAINSBURY, E, *In and Out of Care: The Experiences of Children, Parents and Social Workers*, Batsford, 1986. Report of major ESRC funded study. In-depth interviews of families and social workers at admission, during care and at discharge.

FRATTER, J, THOBURN, J, SAPSFORD, D & ROWE, J, *Outcomes of Family Placement* (forthcoming BAAF). A survey of 'permanent' placements made by voluntary societies with analysis and discussion.

FRATTER, J, *Family Placement and Access: Achieving Permanency for Children in Contact with Birth Parents*, Barnardos, 1989. Based on M.Phil. thesis. Interviews with social workers in 22 voluntary adoption societies and with families where children continued some contact with birth families after legal adoption.

GARNETT, L, *Leaving Care for Independence: A follow up study to the Placement Outcomes Project*. Report to the Department of Health, 1990. An examination of the experiences of 135 young people based on information from social workers.

HAIMES, E & TIMMS, N, *Adoption, Identity and Social Policy*, Gower, 1985. Research on S26 of the Children Act 1975. Postal questionnaires to authorities and interviews with counsellors and adopted people.

HARDWICK, N, 'Asleep on the Streets', *Social Work Today*, 5 July 1990. Brief article on homeless teenagers.

HEATH, A, COLTON, M & ALDGATE, J, 'Educational Progress of Children In and Out of Care', *The British Journal of Social Work*, Vol. 19, No. 6, December 1989. Initial findings from longitudinal study of 49 long-term foster children and comparison group of children receiving social services at home. Interviews and educational and adjustment tests.

HIGGINSON, S, 'Distorted Evidence', *Community Care*, 17 May 1990. Article based on M.Phil. thesis. An intensive examination of 40 case conferences.

82

HOGGAN, P & O'HARA, G, 'Permanent substitute family care in Lothian - placement outcome', *Adoption & Fostering*, Vol. 12, No. 3, 1988. A report on the 335 placements made by Lothian between 1982 and 1987.

HOWE, D & HININGS, D, *The Post-Adoption Centre, First Three Years: Adopted People*, University of East Anglia, September 1989. Part of a comprehensive study of the Centre and its clients.

HUNDLEBY, M, 'The pros and cons of specialisation', *Adoption & Fostering*, Vol. 13, No. 3, 1989. An account of the varied organisational patterns for the adoption and fostering service in the six authorities which took part in the 'Child Care Now' research study.

JACKSON, S, *The Education of Children in Care*, Bristol Papers in Applied Social Studies No. 1, The School of Applied Social Studies, University of Bristol, 1987. A discussion paper.

KAHAN, B, 'The Physical and Mental Health of Children in Care' in KAHAN, B (ed), *Child Care Research, Policy and Practice*, Hodder and Stoughton, 1989. Paper prepared for Open University text.

KEANE, A, 'Behaviour problems among long-term foster children', *Adoption and Fostering*, Vol. 7, No. 3, 1983. Discussion of problems reported by 139 foster families. Based on data from research reported in *Long-Term Foster Care*, Rowe et al, 1984.

KELLY, G, *Patterns of Care: Child care careers and the patterns that shape them*, The Queen's University of Belfast, Department of Social Studies, unpublished report for the DHSS, Northern Ireland, October 1990. A cohort study of 83 children who entered care in Northern Ireland and stayed at least 4 weeks. Follow-up at 12 months. Records and interviews with social workers.

KNAPP, M, BAINES, B & FENYO, A, 'Consistencies and Inconsistencies in Child Care Placements', *British Journal of Social Work*, Vol. 18, Supplement, 1985. A study of placement choice in one authority with consideration of ethnicity among other variables.

LOWE, K, *Teenagers in Foster Care*, NFCA, 1990. A national survey.

MALOS, E & BULLARD, E, *Custodianship: The Care of Other People's Children*, HMSO, 1991 (forthcoming). Research for the Department of Health into the use, and non-use, of custodianship.

MACASKILL, C, *An Evaluation of Parents for Children's Post Adoption Services*, July 1987. A second-round follow-up of families who had adopted children with disabilities. Focus on services used and needed.

MARSH, P, 'Changing practice in child care - The Children Act 1989', *Adoption and Fostering*, Vol. 14, No. 4, 1990. A discussion of the philosophy and practice of partnership and why it is difficult to implement it.

MILLHAM, S, BULLOCK, R, HOSIE, K & LITTLE, M, *Lost in Care: the Problems of Maintaining Links between Children in Care and their Families*, Gower, 1986. A major DHSS funded study of a cohort of 450 children entering care in 1980 and followed up for two years. Records, interviews with social workers and with a small number of families.

MILLHAM ET AL, *Access Disputes in Child-Care*, Gower, 1989. An extensive and intensive study of the effect of the HASSASSA Act (1983) giving parents the right to challenge social work decisions to terminate access. Includes investigation of arrangements for implementation, compares 'de jure' and 'de facto' terminations and examines the efficacy of the Code of Practice.

PACKMAN, J with RANDALL, J & JACQUES, N, *Who Needs Care?* Blackwell, 1986. A DHSS funded research study of decisions about admission to care and their outcomes in two authorities. 361 cases, interviews with social workers and parents.

PACKMAN, J, 'Decisions in Child Care' in KAHAN, B (ed), *Child Care Research, Policy and Practice*, Hodder and Stoughton, 1989. A general discussion of decision making and the child care services.

PARTRIDGE, A, *Young People Leaving Care in Oxford*, Oxfordshire County Council, May 1989. Study commissioned by Oxfordshire County Council. Interviews with 24 young people and with adults providing services for them.

84

ROCKEL, J & RYBURN, M, *Adoption Today: Change and Choice in New Zealand*, Heinemann Reed, 1988. An exploration of experiences and attitudes to adoption with emphasis on open adoption.

ROBBINS, D, see Social Services Inspectorate, *Child Care Policy: Putting It In Writing*, 1990.

ROWE, J, CAIN, H, HUNDLEBY, M & KEANE, A, *Long-Term Foster Care*, Batsford/BAAF, 1984. A DHSS funded, in-depth study of 200 placements based on interviews with foster parents, children, natural parents and social workers.

ROWE, J, HUNDLEBY, M & GARNETT, L, *Child Care Now*, BAAF, Research Series 6, 1989. A large scale survey of over 9,000 placement starts and endings in six authorities. Based on questionnaires completed by social workers.

RUSHTON, A, TRESEDER, J & QUINTON, D, *New parents for older children*, BAAF, Discussion Series 10, 1988. Detailed investigation and follow up of adoption placements of 18 boys aged 5-9 years. Repeated in-depth interviews with new parents and with social workers.

RUSHTON, A, TRESEDER, J & QUINTON, D, 'Sibling groups in permanent placements', *Adoption & Fostering*, Vol. 13, No. 4, 1989. Article exploring the influence of sibling relationships in the placements described in *New parents for older children*.

RUSSELL, J, BROWNLIE, H & FREEMAN, I, *Fostering and Adoption Disruption Research Project: The Temporary Placements*, Scottish Office, February 1988. Examination of foster placements that lasted at least four weeks but not intended to be long-term. Records and interviews with all participants.

SHAW, M & HIPGRAVE, T, 'Specialist Fostering 1988 - A research study', *Adoption and Fostering*, Vol. 13, No. 3, 1989. The first of two articles reporting on a new survey updating previous research.

SOCIAL SERVICES INSPECTORATE, DHSS, *Inspection of Community Homes*, September 1985. A detailed and critical review of residential services based on extended visits to 149 homes.

SOCIAL SERVICES INSPECTORATE, DHSS, *Inspection of the Supervision of Social Workers in the Assessment and Monitoring of Cases of Child Abuse When Children, Subject to a Court Order, Have Been Returned Home*, DHSS Summary Report, March 1986. An inspection resulting from the Jasmine Beckford enquiry. Covered 117 cases in nine authorities.

SOCIAL SERVICES INSPECTORATE, DH, *A Sense of Direction: Planning in Social Work with Children*, HMSO, 1989. A synthesis of SSI inspection reports with evaluations of child care policy and practice.

SOCIAL SERVICES INSPECTORATE, DH, *Child Care Policy: Putting It In Writing*, HMSO, 1990. A comprehensive review and analysis of local authority child care policy documents with suggestions.

SOCIAL SERVICES INSPECTORATE, DH, *Inspection of Child Protection Services in Rochdale*, Social Services Inspectorate North Western Region, October 1990. A study undertaken at the request of the authority at a time of public concern.

STALKER, K, *'Share the Care': An Evaluation of a Family-Based Respite Care Service*, Jessica Kingsley Publishers, 1990. Research into respite care scheme in Lothian for children with learning difficulties. Interviews with parents and carers.

STEIN, M & CAREY, K, *Leaving Care*, Blackwell, 1986. An enquiry into the experiences and problems of care leavers based on a series of interviews over a 2 year period with 45 young people in Wakefield.

STONE, J, *Children in Care: The Role of Short-Term Fostering*, Adoption and Fostering Unit, City of Newcastle Upon Tyne Social Services, October 1990. Examination of 104 placements based on information from social workers and records. Discusses variations in use and outcome.

SWANSON, M, 'Preventing Reception into Care: Monitoring a Short-Stay Refuge for Older Children', in *Research Highlights in Social Work* 17, (eds.), FREEMAN, I & MONTGOMERY, S Kingsley, 1988. Report on an innovative resource developed by Strathclyde Regional Council.

THOBURN, J, 'What kind of permanence?' *Adoption and Fostering*, Vol. 9, No. 4, 1985. An article discussing the many routes to permanent placements with or without family contact.

THOBURN, J, *Success and Failure in Permanent Family Placement*, Avebury, 1990. A follow-up after five years of the 21 children previously studied. Includes a full review of the literature on permanent placements.

THOBURN, J, MURDOCH, A & O'BRIEN, A, *Permanence in Child Care*, Blackwell, 1986. A detailed study of one adoption agency and the 'special needs' placements it made, with follow-up after two years. Interviews with adopters, children and social workers.

THOBURN, J & ROWE, J, 'Research: A snapshot of permanent family placement', *Adoption & Fostering*, Vol. 12, No. 3, 1988. Report of a survey of over a thousand 'special needs' children placed by voluntary agencies.

THORPE, D, 'Career Patterns in Child Care - Implications for Service', *British Journal of Social Work*, Vol. 18, No. 2, 1988. An article based on a study of child care in Leicestershire.

TRENT, J, *Homeward Bound: The Rehabilitation of Children to Their Birth Parents*, Barnardo's New Families Project, March 1989. An intensive study of the rehabilitation of 36 children who had originally been referred for adoptive placement.

TRISELIOTIS, J & RUSSELL, J, *Hard to Place: The Outcome of Adoption and Residential Care*, ESRC/DHSS Studies in Deprivation and Disadvantage, Heinemann Educational Books, 1984. A comparison of outcomes of late adoptions and long-term residential care based on interviews with adults. The effects of early adversity and inter-generational links are also considered.

VALLENDER, I, 'Family Centres - Who Needs Them?', *Concern*, No. 74, Autumn 1990. Brief article looking at family centres in the light of the Children Act requirement that centres be provided 'as appropriate'.

VON ARNIM, I, *Fostering Adolescents: Effects on the Host Children*. Dissertation submitted for the M.Sc. in Applied Social Studies, Oxford University, June 1988. Interviews with 11 families with 'own' children aged 8-12 and experience of fostering adolescents.

WEBB, S, 'Preventing reception into care: a literature review of respite care', *Adoption & Fostering*, Vol. 14, No. 2, 1990. An article based on work for a feasibility study of respite care.

WEDGE, P & MANTLE, G, *Sibling Groups and Social Work*, Avebury Gower, 1991 (forthcoming). A study of sibling groups referred for permanent placement and the outcome of the placements.

WEDGE, P & PHELAN, J, 'The Impossible Demands of Child Care' and 'Moving Toward a Wider Range of Foster Homes', *Social Work Today*, Vol. 19, Nos. 35 and 39. Articles reporting on data from a study of child care in Essex.

WEDGE, S, *Growing Up Alone: Final Report*, Trust for the Study of Adolescence, unpublished report, 1988. A small, in-depth study based on 32 interviews with young people who were or had been in a therapeutic residential setting. Explores feelings and attitudes toward parents, carers and other sources of support.

WHITAKER, D ET AL, *The Experience of Residential Care from the Perspectives of Children, Parents and Caregivers*, Dept of Administration and Social Work, University of York. An ESRC sponsored study which focused on 34 children, and their care givers, parents and social workers.

WILTSHIRE COUNTY COUNCIL SOCIAL SERVICES, *Children in Care*, 1990. A self-study undertaken in one division of the county with emphasis on planning.

YATES, P, *Post-Placement Support for Adoptive Families of Hard-to-Place Children*, M.Sc. thesis, Edinburgh, 1985. Small scale study based on interviews with adopters and social workers.

PART FIVE WHAT IS YOUR EVIDENCE?

This section offers some working tools for practice. There are checklists, questionnaires and group or individual exercises which are all designed to be of interest and use to practitioners and managers. All are concerned with some aspect of the gathering or weighing up of evidence - the evidence upon which child care services should be planned and decisions should be made. All arise from issues which have been highlighted in research reports and discussed in previous sections.

Some of these tools are simple but carefully designed questionnaires for gathering data through a team or agency survey e.g. the racial and cultural background of a group of children. Others offer suggestions for examining a behaviour problem in depth or looking at the relationships of siblings. Others again are intended to stimulate thought and self examination of attitudes or the discharge of particular responsibilities, e.g. dissemination of policy and procedure papers. Some of the checklists and questionnaires can be used cumulatively to gather data on an important topic e.g. the needs of young people moving into independence or barriers to family contact.

It is hoped that readers will use these various tools flexibly and imaginatively. There is no suggestion that anyone should attempt all of them. They are presented in the order in which the topic appears in the text and people may wish to adapt them for particular uses. The aim is to stimulate thought and discussion, reinforce important messages from the research studies and offer some interesting ways of getting to grips with problems Although they are essentially intended for day to day practice, most of these tools provide useful exercises for study days or training courses. Copies of those which may need to be duplicated will be found in the pocket at the back of this publication.

Any exercise or enquiry which effectively challenges existing ways of doing or thinking can all too easily be perceived as inquisitorial and put people on the defensive. Becoming defensive inevitably means closing one's mind to new options. This means that if trainers and managers want staff to be open and questioning about their practice, it is essential to avoid presenting any of these tools as though they were a management device for checking up on performance. That is very far from the intention. They are meant to build up skill and confidence by helping people to develop a secure basis for their decisions and judgements.

READY TO COPE ALONE?

A personal balance sheet for a young person who will move into independent living

(These questionnaires have been developed in consultation with Tory Laughland, Editor of 'Who Cares?' and Harriet Ward, Secretary to the Department of Health Working Party on the Assessment of Outcomes in Child Care.)

Note: Although 'independent living' is the phrase commonly used, it is important to remember how inappropriate it really is. Most 18 year olds are not expected to do without considerable family support and 'interdependence' is the capacity most needed in adult life.

Purpose

These two questionnaires - one for the young person to complete and a supplementary one for adults - offer a method of taking stock of a young person's readiness to move on into adult life and to manage alone. Although they are focussed on those young people who will be moving out to live independently, minor modifications will make them suitable for use with any 15 to 18 year old. They can be particularly helpful when used just before an important review or planning meeting and when completed they provide a basis for deciding:

● **what level of independence is appropriate and whether it should be a staged process;**

● **the optimum timing for such a move;**

● **the practical things that need to be done;**

● **the 'gaps' in personal development or experience for which remedial action should be planned**.

It is highly desirable to start this stock-taking well before a move becomes imminent. This will make it possible to take the necessary steps to ensure that the youngster has a reasonable chance of managing successfully. It may be necessary to complete the questionnaires more than once if the first round shows that there is a lot still to be done.

Although primarily designed to gather information on individuals, regular use of the questionnaires would build up a picture of the department's care leavers. Answers to the key questions could be extracted and analysed and this would provide essential evidence about what is needed and help with the planning and monitoring of leaving care schemes.

Method

The main check list is for the young person· to complete. There is always a risk that youngsters will find it depressing or upsetting to look in depth at their situation and their limited experience and resources. However, it is better to face the problem while still in a familiar and supportive environment than to move out unprepared. Care and thought will be needed in deciding the appropriate moment to use the questionnaires. They should always be presented and explained by a trusted adult and though some young people may prefer to complete them on their own, others will find it easier to make it a joint effort with their social worker or other well known adult. Either way, it will be important for the young person and the adults who have worked on the supplementary questionnaire, to talk over the answers to the questions ahead of the review or meeting at which decisions about independent living will be made. The completed profile can then form the basis for open discussion, plans can be agreed to deal with any practical problems which have been identified and consideration given to how any serious gaps in development or experience can best be made up.

The young person's own wishes, hopes and anxieties should be centre stage at this point e.g. Does s/he want to move? His or her participation in the review is, of course, essential as is that of current (and perhaps past) carers. In most cases it will also be helpful to include parents or other relatives.

It should go without saying that copies of the completed questionnaire should not be made or distributed without the young person's express permission.

READY TO COPE ALONE?

This questionnaire is intended to help you to make good plans for living independently. It looks rather long, but that is because there are so many important things to be considered. It is worth taking some time and trouble over the questions. They will help you to think about what it will be like to manage your own affairs, what you need to know or find out about and what may still have to be done in order to make sure that you have a good chance of making a success of your life.

Try to answer all the questions but don't hesitate to ask for help if you need it. There may be some questions which you can't answer yet. (For example, you may not yet know how much money you will have or what your rent will be.) If you don't know the answer, just put a question mark to remind yourself that this is something that you will want to ask about.

Fill in the blank spaces or put a ring round the words that best describe your situation or your plans:

....

Your name   Your age now

I Practical Arrangements

Accommodation

1   Where do you plan to live after you leave your present home?

   ....

2a If you will be living in a flat or bedsit, is the furniture and equipment
   adequate?

   | Yes | 1 |
   | No | 2 |

2b Think about cooking, cleaning and heating arrangements. Will you have
   enough bedding, china, pots and pans? How about a radio or TV?

   | Yes | 1 |
   | No | 2 |

   If no, what else do you need?

   ....

   ....

Money

1a How much money will you have each week?   £ ....

1b Where will this money come from? (e.g. wages, grant, DHSS) ....

2 What will your expenses be?   £   p

Rent

....

Gas

....

Electricity

....

Food

....

Fares

....

Clothes

....

Entertainment
   (e.g. TV Licence)

....

Other Things

....

TOTAL

....

3a Will your income cover your expenses?

Yes	1
No	2

3b If no, what can you do about this?

....

....

II Education and Employment

1 Did you pass any exams at school or college?

| Yes 1 |
| No 2 |

If yes, what were they?

....

....

2 Have you had any skills training?

| Yes 1 |
| No 2 |

If yes, to what level?

....

....

3 Have you had any work experience?

| Yes 1 |
| No 2 |

If yes, what was it and for how long?

....

....

4 Which of these do you have:

A job?

| Yes 1 |
| No 2 |

A place in further education?

| Yes 1 |
| No 2 |

A place on a training course?

| Yes 1 |
| No 2 |

None of these?

| Yes 1 |
| No 2 |

5   If you have a job or a place on a training course, is it:

Full-Time

| Yes 1 |
| No 2 |

Part-Time

| Yes 1 |
| No 2 |

Temporary

| Yes 1 |
| No 2 |

Regular

| Yes 1 |
| No 2 |

6   Do you have any other qualifications that might help you to get a job (e.g. typing, computer skills)?

| Yes 1 |
| No 2 |

If yes, what are they?

....

....

7   Do you have a driving licence?

| Yes 1 |
| No 2 |

8   Do you know how to write a letter applying for a job?

| Yes 1 |
| No 2 |

If no, would you like some help with this?

| Yes 1 |
| No 2 |

9   Would you like some advice about how to present yourself in a job interview?

| Yes 1 |
| No 2 |

III Health

1   When did you last have a medical check-up?

....

2   When did you last have a dental check-up?

....

3   If you wear glasses, do you need to see an optician?

| Yes 1 |
| No 2 |

4   Do you feel able to arrange these appointments and go to them by yourself?

| Yes 1 |
| No 2 |

5   If you have a chronic health problem (like asthma or diabetes) do you feel that you know enough about how to deal with it?

Yes	1
No	2
Does not apply 3	

6   Do you know how to get help if you feel ill or get hurt?

| Yes 1 |
| No 2 |

7   Do you think you have had enough opportunities to discuss the following with an adult whom you trust?

    a   Sexual relationships and responsibilities?

| Yes 1 |
| No 2 |

    b   How you feel about having children?

| Yes 1 |
| No 2 |

    c   The risk of getting AIDS?

| Yes 1 |
| No 2 |

    d   How to practice safe sex?

| Yes 1 |
| No 2 |

    e   How to cope with racial discrimination or sexual harassment?

| Yes 1 |
| No 2 |

8   Would you like more information about any of these?

| Yes 1 |
| No 2 |

IV Useful Life Skills

1   Which of the following have you ever done?

    a   Cooked a proper meal (not just fried eggs etc)

| Yes 1 |
| No 2 |

b   Turned up a skirt hem or trouser leg

Yes 1
No ?

c   Fitted an electric plug on an appliance

Yes 1
No 2

d   Filled up a claim form

Yes 1
No 2

e   Used a public telephone

Yes 1
No 2

f   Opened a bank account or post office savings account

Yes 1
No 2

g   Dealt with a blocked sink

Yes 1
No 2

h   Saved up to buy something that you could not afford to buy straight
    away

Yes 1
No 2

Yes 1
No 2

i   Used a launderette

Yes 1
No 2

Yes 1
No 2

2   Do you know:

a   How to use a bus or train timetable and plan a journey

Yes 1
No 2

b   How to register with a dentist/doctor

Yes 1
No 2

c   How to get legal advice

Yes 1
No 2

d   Where to go for information about your welfare rights

Yes 1
No 2

e   Where to go for contraceptive supplies and advice

Yes 1
No 2

3   Do you know where to find:

a   Your birth certificate

Yes 1
No 2

b   Your national insurance number

Yes 1
No 2

c   Your national health service card

Yes 1
No 2

V Family and Friends

1 Do you have a family home base (either your own family or a foster family) or a former children's home or unit, where you will feel welcome and where you can:

a Be sure of a bed if necessary

Yes 1
No 2

b Expect to go for major holidays such as Christmas

Yes 1
No 2

c Drop in without an invitation if you are bored or lonely

Yes 1
No 2

d Expect help at special times such as your wedding, when you have your first child or if some crisis occurs

Yes 1
No 2

2 a How often are you in contact with the following members of your own family or your foster family?

	Weekly	Monthly	Sometimes	Never	Does not Apply
Mother					
Father					
Brother/Sister					
Grandparent(s)					
Relatives					
Family Friends					

b Do you have addresses for these people

Yes 1
No 2

c Is this amount of contact about right for you or would you like it to be different? more? less?

....

d Would you like some help with this?

Yes 1
No 2

3   Is there at least one adult (in addition to your social worker), who you feel you could go to for help, advice and support if a problem comes up?

| Yes 1 |
| No 2 |

4   (If you come from a minority ethnic group.) Do you have good friends at present who share the same culture/first language/religion as you?

| Yes 1 |
| No 2 |

5   Do you have at least one close friend with whom you can keep in touch after you move?

| Yes 1 |
| No 2 |

6   Do you belong to any club, team, church or other organisation?

| Yes 1 |
| No 2 |

    If no, would you like to?

| Yes 1 |
| No 2 |

7   Will you be living in a neighbourhood that you know well?

| Yes 1 |
| No 2 |

8   Will you be living near people of the same ethnic group/first language/religion as you?

| Yes 1 |
| No 2 |

VI Personal Strengths and Resources

1   a   Do you have detailed knowledge of your family background and your own life history?

| Yes 1 |
| No 2 |

    b   Do you know who will be able to help you to get more information if you want it?

| Yes 1 |
| No 2 |

2   a   Have you decided what to say about your life so far if officials ask questions or when you have to fill in the personal details on forms?

| Yes 1 |
| No 2 |

    b   Would it help to discuss this with somebody?

| Yes 1 |
| No 2 |

3   a   Do you have a hobby or special interest?

| Yes 1 |
| No 2 |

    b   If yes, do you have the equipment you need for it?

| Yes 1 |
| No 2 |

4   Have you thought about how you are going to spend your spare time?

| Yes 1 |
| No 2 |

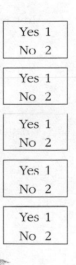

5   a   How well will you be able to cope with loneliness?

....

....

b   Have you got some ideas about how to overcome loneliness? What are they?

....

....

....

c   Do you know where to go for help if you feel really bad?

Yes	1
No	2

6   What do you think you might do if you want to make some new friends?

....

....

....

....

Pause here and look back over your answers so far. It may be a good idea to discuss them with someone you respect and trust before you try to answer the next three questions.

VII Summing Up

1   How ready do you feel to manage living on your own?

Ready now	1
Not quite yet but soon	2
Not yet	3

2   What are your strong points?

....

....

3   What are your weaker points?

....

....

Signature   ....

Date   ....

VII What Next?

There will probably be quite a lot of things that still need to be done. It is important to make a plan and decide what you will do yourself and what your social worker or other adults will do for you or with you. Use the questionnaire to make a list for discussion with your social worker and also at your next review. Try to cover all the topics: accommodation, money, education and employment, health, family and friends, personal resources. Write down what has to be done, who will do it and when.

Good luck.

Ready to Cope Alone?

A supplementary checklist for key adults

This questionnaire is intended to be used in parallel with the one for the young person. When completed, it should be discussed with the young person in preparation for the review or conference at which plans for preparation for independent living will be drawn up.

....

Young person's name   Age now

....

When last admitted   Number of addresses since then

1   Health and Development

a   Does s/he have any disability or health problems that should be taken into consideration in planning for independent living?

> Yes 1
> No 2

If yes, what ....

b   Are you satisfied that s/he has had sufficient access to advice on safe sex, drugs, smoking, alcohol etc.

> Yes 1
> No 2

2 Accommodation

a   Is the accommodation to which s/he is moving intended to be temporary or long term?

b   If temporary, is there a definite prospect of long term accommodation?

> Yes 1
> No 2

c   If yes, what? .... When? ....

d   If no, who will be responsible for finding something suitable? ....

3 Finances

a   Will his/her income be:

| above benefit level |
| at benefit level |
| below benefit level |

b   Will this income be sufficient to enable him/her to function normally?

| Yes 1 |
| No 2 |

c   If no, what plan can be made to supplement it?

....

d   What financial costs to the department (one-off and on-going) are involved in setting
    up and maintaining this young person in independent living?

....

e   How can this money be obtained? ....

4 Nationality and Ethnic Issues

a   Is s/he of full British nationality?

| Yes 1 |
| No 2 |

b   If no, what steps need to be taken to regularise and, if necessary, safeguard his/her
    immigration, citizenship and nationality status? ....

....

c   Has all this been discussed with him/her?

| Yes 1 |
| No 2 |

d   Does s/he have all the documents s/he may need for future dealings over
    passport, immigration etc?

| Yes 1 |
| No 2 |

e   (If the young person is black or from a minority ethnic group) Are you satisfied that
    s/he has had opportunities to:

   i   know people of the same racial or ethnic background

   ii   learn about his/her cultural background

   iii discuss racism, prejudice and discrimination and ways of dealing with them.

5 Summing Up

a   Do you agree with the young person's self assessment of his/her
    readiness for independent living?

    | Yes 1 |
    | No 2 |

b   If no, what is your opinion? ....

    ....

c   How much social work support is needed and acceptable to this youngster? ....

    Who will provide it? ....

d   If support is needed but is not acceptable at present, what contingency plans can be
    put in place to provide it later if requested? ....

    ....

    Signature .... Date ....

You may find it helpful to use the attached work sheet in discussion with the young person
and/or at the review. It is important to reach agreement not only on what needs to be done,
but who will do it, how and when.

Agreed Plan of Preparation for Independence

What needs to be done?	Who will do it?	How?	When?

RACIAL AND CULTURAL BACKGROUND. A CENSUS

Purpose

This brief questionnaire provides a means of gathering basic information for planning services which take account of racial origin, religion, language and cultural background and thus conform to S22(5)(c) of the Children Act 1989. It can be used to cover either large or small groups e.g. all children being 'looked after' by the authority, or just those in one area or one team. Alternatively, the enquiry could focus on a particular group of children e.g. those in foster homes or in residential establishments.

Although it is primarily designed as a tool for a census, the questionnaire could quite well be used routinely for all admissions. This would ensure that the relevant information on race, religion and language is recorded and available for all children. The information is sufficiently detailed for effective planning and should also serve as a reminder that cultural differences are not confined to ethnic issues - important though these are. For instance, Irish children may experience a distinct culture at home. It will also serve as a reminder that when considering children of mixed parentage and their needs, it is necessary to know not only the background of each parent, but also the ethnic and cultural background in which the child has been living. Parents' requests regarding cultural and religious observances should be recorded and taken seriously.

Method

A questionnaire should be completed for each child or young person in the sample group on a specified date. The results can be analysed by computer, or by hand if the sample is small - less than a hundred.

Completing these forms offers an opportunity for social workers to:

- check out how well they know the background and needs of 'their' children

- consider the appropriateness of current or proposed placements

- think about the parents' expectations and anxieties

- foresee potential problems for minority group parents in communicating and entering into a partnership with carers and social workers.

Racial and Cultural Background - a Census

Child's Name ....   **Case Number** ....

Sex   Male   1   **Age** (yrs) ....
          Female 2   (If less than 1 yr=00)

1 Ethnic background

	Mother	Father
White - Eng., Welsh, Scot	1	1
White - Irish	2	2
White - Other	3	3
Carribean	4	4
African	5	5
Indian	6	6
Pakistani	7	7
Bangladeshi	8	8
Chinese	9	9
Arab	10	10
Other	11	11
Not Known	12	12

If other please specify ....

2 With whom was the child living when at home?

Both Parents   1
Mother   2
Father   3   If other relative/family
Other Relative 4   friend please specify
Family Friend   5

....

3 What is the child's nationality?

British   1   If other please specify
Other   2

....

4 Predominant language spoken at home (add other languages generally spoken in your area e.g. Welsh or African languages)

English	1
Bengali	2
Urdu	3
Punjabi	4
Gujarati	5
Other	6

If other please specify

....

5 If the language spoken at home is not English, which members:

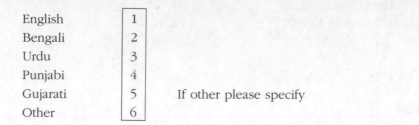

	Speak English	Read & write English
Child		
Mother		
Father		
Other Relative Specify		

....

6 Child's religion - select one

None	1	Seventh Day Adventist	8
Roman Catholic	2	Jewish	9
Church of England	3	Moslem	10
Other Protestant	4	Hindu	11
Pentecostal	5	Sikh	12
Rastafarian	6	Other	13
Jehovah's Witness	7	Not known	14

If other please specify ....

7 Does the child practise his/her religion at home?

| Yes | 1 |
| No | 2 |

8 Do the parents have any special requests and if so what?

A   About the child's food?

....

B   About the child's clothes?

....

C   About religious observances?

....

D   About other matters?

....

SIBLING RELATIONSHIPS - A CHECK LIST
(Based on material from The Bridge Child Care Consultancy Service)

Note: The term 'sibling' should be interpreted quite widely to include adopted, step and half sibs, foster sibs, cousins or other relatives who may have been brought up with the child whose needs are being considered, and even close friends. The latter may be more important to a child than siblings whom s/he has never met. Research has shown that sibling relationships are very important but apt to be overlooked.

Purpose

This is a basic tool for studying the way siblings behave toward each other and through this coming to a better understanding of their relationship. It is not primarily a means of deciding whether siblings should be placed together, and though it should form one part of the evidence gathered for such a decision, it should not be used as the only basis for that decision.

It can appropriately be used on behalf of children in a wide variety of family or residential settings where sibling relationships are causing concern or need to be better understood as part of future planning. It could, for instance, be part of a study of relationships on access visits.

The aim is to avoid the ever present risk of making unwarranted assumptions or drawing false conclusions from partial or biased evidence. This is why the check list focusses on actual, observed behaviour and it is essential to back up each statement with an example.

It can be helpful to compare relationships over time and in different settings, so notes about changes and whether a particular behaviour is only recent or of very long standing, may be illuminating. But the list should focus on the present.

Psychologists such as Judy Dunn have shown that behaviour patterns between sibs tend to be rather stable. However, the placement changes which occur when children are looked after by local authorities, may provide opportunities to modify relationships quite profoundly. They can also put relationships under extra strain.

Who Should Be Involved

This check list must be completed by people with first-hand knowledge of the children. Hearsay evidence will not do.

If the siblings are separated, they would have to be brought together for some of the assessment and some additional questions would be useful e.g. Do they try to keep in touch?

It may be appropriate for carers (past or present) to complete the check lists on their own or just with a social worker. However, very good results can be obtained by working on the lists in a group containing both past and present carers (including parents), the social worker(s), and any other people who are closely involved with the children as a sibling group. The presence of those who have observed the children at different times and in different settings helps to ensure a balanced picture and gives an opportunity to challenge allegations and assumptions. When it comes to the analysis, a group is really essential.

Completing the Lists

Relationships are always two-way. What may be mainly positive for one sib may be very mixed or even mainly negative for the other. This means that it is important to look at each piece of behaviour from each child's point of view and then go on to consider more general aspects of their inter-action. All three parts of the list should be completed for each sibling pair. If there are several children in the family, the main features of each pair relationship can be brought together on a diagram using coloured pencils to denote positive, negative etc.

It is better to leave a question unanswered than to complete it on inadequate evidence. However, too many blank answers will indicate the need for further observation.

If a behaviour is found to vary greatly, it may be necessary to give several examples with details of circumstances. A pattern may then emerge.

Analysing and Interpreting the Check List

The first step is to examine the recorded behaviours identifying those which appear to be positive and which negative but remembering that both are present in all sibling relationships. The balance in this relationship will probably become evident, but it may be somewhat different or more complex than carers had previously realised.

Some types of behaviour have been found to have more significance than others in differentiating between a rich or a poor relationship. For example, sharing in boisterous play, resolving conflict through age-appropriate reasoning and reciprocal attempts to alleviate distress, all seem to have special importance. The latter may be particularly relevant for siblings who have shared the experience of separation from adult carers.

When attempting to interpret the meaning of the behaviour which has been observed and recorded and to understand this relationship, it is important to bear in mind the whole context in which this relationship has developed. Aspects to be considered include:

● The children's position in the family - a simple family tree may help here

● gender

● cultural and family expectations for each child

● the emotional age at which each is functioning

● the extent to which the children have a shared history and family experience

● the role each child is perceived to have played (if any), in the sibling group's admission to care or accommodation.

The deeper and more accurate understanding which should emerge from the analysis will provide a more secure basis for making decisions about the children's future, for devising work programmes to meet their individual needs and for effective support for carers in managing and modifying behaviour.

SIBLING RELATIONSHIP CHECK LIST 1

Child A .... DOB ....

Child B .... DOB ....

Behaviour of child A to child B	frequency (select one)

A   Defends or protects
      examples of this behaviour:

1	Often
2	Sometimes
3	Never

....

....

B   Recognises sib's distress and offers comfort
      examples of this behaviour:

1	Often
2	Sometimes
3	Never

....

....

C   Accepts comfort from sib
      examples of this behaviour:

1	Often
2	Sometimes
3	Never

....

....

D   Teaches or helps
      examples of this behaviour:

1	Often
2	Sometimes
3	Never

....

....

E Initiates play
   examples of this behaviour:

1	Often
2	Sometimes
3	Never

....

....

F Responds to overtures to play
   examples of this behaviour:

1	Often
2	Sometimes
3	Never

....

....

G Openly shows affection
   examples of this behaviour:

1	Often
2	Sometimes
3	Never

....

....

H Misses sib when apart
   examples of this behaviour:

1	Often
2	Sometimes
3	Never

....

....

I Resolves conflict through age-appropriate reasoning
   examples of this behaviour:

1	Often
2	Sometimes
3	Never

....

....

J   Annoys, irritates or teases
examples of this behaviour:

1	Often
2	Sometimes
3	Never

....

....

K   Shows hostility or agression
examples of this behaviour:

1	Often
2	Sometimes
3	Never

....

....

L   Blames or attempts to get sib into trouble
examples of this behaviour:

1	Often
2	Sometimes
3	Never

....

....

M   Behaviour sabotages efforts to meet other sib's needs
examples of this behaviour:

1	Often
2	Sometimes
3	Never

....

....

SIBLING RELATIONSHIP CHECK LIST 2

Child B .... **DOB** ....

Child A .... **DOB** ....

Behaviour of child B to child A	frequency (select one)

A Defends or protects
examples of this behaviour:

1	Often
2	Sometimes
3	Never

....

....

B Recognises sib's distress and offers comfort
examples of this behaviour:

1	Often
2	Sometimes
3	Never

....

....

C Accepts comfort from sib
examples of this behaviour:

1	Often
2	Sometimes
3	Never

....

....

D Teaches or helps
examples of this behaviour:

1	Often
2	Sometimes
3	Ncvcr

....

....

E   Initiates play
     examples of this behaviour:

1	Often
2	Sometimes
3	Never

....

....

F   Responds to overtures to play
     examples of this behaviour:

1	Often
2	Sometimes
3	Never

....

....

G   Openly shows affection
     examples of this behaviour:

1	Often
2	Sometimes
3	Never

....

....

H   Misses sib when apart
     examples of this behaviour:

1	Often
2	Sometimes
3	Never

....

....

I   Resolves conflict through age-appropriate reasoning
     examples of this behaviour:

1	Often
2	Sometimes
3	Never

....

....

J   Annoys, irritates or teases
    examples of this behaviour:

1	Often
2	Sometimes
3	Never

....

....

K   Shows hostility or agression
    examples of this behaviour:

1	Often
2	Sometimes
3	Never

....

....

L   Blames or attempts to get sib into trouble
    examples of this behaviour:

1	Often
2	Sometimes
3	Never

....

....

M   Behaviour sabotages efforts to meet other sib's needs
    examples of this behaviour:

1	Often
2	Sometimes
3	Never

....

....

SIBLING CHECKLIST 3

Interactions

1 What evidence is there of sharing:

....

	Examples
Boisterous play	
Imaginative activities	
Rituals (e.g. bed or bath time)	
Jokes and fun	
Secrets	
Other	

2 Are there marked differences between them in any of the following respects:

....

	Examples
The roles they adopt	
Activities and interests	
Behaviour	
Personality	
Other	

3 What evidence is there of reciprocity e.g.

....

	Examples
Pride in each other	
Praise and criticism	
Mutual help	

4   Do they model on each other e.g.

....

Examples

....

Think they look alike

....

Imitate each other

....

Emulate the qualities
they like

....

Unite in face of
problems

....

Other

....

5   Other observations on this relationship ....

....

....

6   What are these siblings' own views of their relationship? (views of other siblings can
also be very illuminating).

....

....

....

**7   On the basis of all this evidence, sum up the positives and negatives that this
relationship holds for each sib.**

....

....

....

Date check list completed ....

How Many Barriers to Parental Contact?

Purpose

The Children Act 1989 requires every social services department and every social worker to pay careful attention to family contact. This simple exercise is a tool which teams or individuals can use to start this process by examining the evidence from their own cases. The questionnaire offers:

a) a systematic way of discovering current visiting levels

b) a means of checking for the presence of some possible barriers to contact which have been identified in research studies but which may not have been recognised in these particular cases.

For the sake of clarity and simplicity, the questionnaire focusses mainly on contact with parents, but it can easily be extended or repeated, to include the wider family.

Some barriers to contact between parents and children are obvious. Others are much less so though they may well account for infrequent visits, phone calls or letters because rather minor difficulties can accumulate to create quite formidable obstacles. Until patterns of contact have been examined in the context of these barriers, it is unwise to draw conclusions about parents' feelings toward their children. Superficial evidence can be misleading and it may be much too simplistic to equate levels of contact with levels of concern. Another advantage of obtaining accurate and detailed information about barriers is that if any are discovered, steps can be taken to remove them. Increased understanding of the effort parents may have to make to achieve even infrequent visits, may result in considerable changes in the attitudes of carers and social workers.

Some of the Ways in which the Questionnaire can be Used

1. To build up an accurate picture of current levels of contact across a series of cases. (The sample could be all children in care or accommodation; all children in one residential establishment; all foster children; all those in long-term care etc.)

2. To review the possible reasons for a lower than desirable level of contact in a particular case where this is causing concern and then take steps to remove any barriers that are identified.

3. To check out social workers' perceptions of what is creating barriers by completing the questionnaire with the parent(s). It is important to recognise that social workers as well as parents and carers can have problems over contact because of the pain that is so often involved.

PARENTAL CONTACT

Child or young person's name ....

Age (yrs) ....

Type of placement ....

Legal status ....

1   What is the present agreement/expectation on frequency of contact for:

Mother ....

Father ....

2   Has anyone made certain that the parents understand and agree with this?

| Yes 1 |
| No 2 |

3   How often have the child and parents actually made contact *during the past two months*?

	Mother	Father	Other Relatives (Specify)
Visits			
Telephone calls			
Letters or cards			
Presents			

4   Has a court laid down any limitation on contact?

| Yes 1 |
| No 2 |

If yes, what limitations and for whom?

....

....

....

Have there been any changes in circumstance or attitudes since these
limitations were imposed?

Yes	1
No	2

5 **Are there any other specific limitations** e.g. specified days or times for
visits or telephone calls? Permitted frequency? Who may visit?

Yes	1
No	2

If yes, what are these and are they still necessary?

....

....

....

If no, does this mean that the parents can (within reason) see their child
whenever they wish? What arrangements do they have to make?

Yes	1
No	2

Arrangements: ....

....

....

Note: The answers to the following questions are bound to be subjective but there will be
less risk of bias or of overlooking barriers if there is discussion with parents or colleagues
in an atmosphere which is both supportive and yet challenges ideas and attitudes.

6 **Are any of the following relevant?**

Scoring: 1   for a minor problem
             2   for a major problem

(If mother and father are living together, do not combine their total score. Visits are often
more difficult when parents are separated.)

	Mother	**Father**
A Distance		
B Transport problems		
C Care of other children		

D	Finance - cost of travel	☐	☐
E	Costs of gifts, food, entertainment during visits	☐	☐
F	Parents' work schedule does not fit with visiting times	☐	☐
G	Parents or carers are not on the telephone	☐	☐
H	Parents find letter writing difficult	☐	☐
I	Child too young to use telephone or write	☐	☐
J	Child refuses contact	☐	☐
K	Carers do not encourage frequent contact	☐	☐
L	Parent has been asked to 'let the child settle'	☐	☐
M	No opportunity for parent to play with child during visits	☐	☐
N	Major class, ethnic or culture difference between carers and parents	☐	☐
O	Parent is upset by child's distress during visit	☐	☐
P	Parent is upset by child's apparent indifference	☐	☐
Q	Carers are upset by child's distress during or after visits	☐	☐
R	Parents and social worker have differing views about contact	☐	☐
S	Parents do not understand/accept why child has to be away from home	☐	☐
T	Dispute between natural parents over contact	☐	☐
U	No social worker available to help arrange visits	☐	☐
V	Other (specify)	☐	☐

....

....

Score   ☐ ☐

GETTING TO GRIPS WITH A PROBLEM BY ANALYSING OBSERVED BEHAVIOUR AND SETTING IT IN CONTEXT

(Based on material from The Bridge Child Care Consultancy Service)

Purpose

The aim of this tool is to identify and understand the root cause of a behaviour problem and, in the process, to increase skills in the collection and analysis of evidence which forms the basis for assessment. Without some structured method of this sort, there is a real risk that both staff and carers will make wrong assumptions.

This tool is presented in relation to an eating problem but it is a technique which can easily be adapted for use with a wide variety of behaviour difficulties. The method of analysis will be the same. It can be used on behalf of children of any age who are being looked after in a foster family or a residential establishment or are living at home. It can also be very useful in Family Centres.

Method

The task is to:

- examine all aspects of the behaviour.
- set it in the context of the child's development, health, life history and family background
- try to make sense of these findings
- plan a work programme to deal with the problem by meeting identified needs

The people involved should include:

all present carers

the child's parents (important, to be strongly encouraged)

past carers (even if problem did not occur then)

others with whom behaviour occurs, e.g. baby sitter, teacher

the social worker(s) responsible for the case

a chairperson and/or a consultant

a health professional

Timing

More than one session may be needed especially if it becomes clear that vital contributors are not present or that past history or background information is inadequate and must be gathered.

If this happens, an interim work programme should be drawn up specifying who will do what before the next meeting. Mealtime behaviour may have to be observed for two or three weeks as a diary or log is essential.

Labels and mind sets

As the child's current eating behaviour is explored, it may become clear that the carers have a very accurate perception of both the child and the behaviour pattern. Alternatively, it may emerge that some or all of the adults involved have an image of the behaviour which does not correspond to present realities. Changes or patterns of behaviour may not have been recognised because people have developed a particular image of the child.

Stereotyping of behaviour is common but unhelpful. The family or staff group may have labelled the child and created a mind-set in their expectations and explanation about what goes on. Personal experiences, values and attitudes are inevitably involved with issues about food. They need to be brought out into the open and may be modified through the discussions, but criticism - especially by the chair or consultant - is not appropriate.

The aim of the questions is to establish whether there are any patterns in the observed behaviour or links with past and present experiences and relationships. Thought should be given to whether the behaviour (or parts of it) is age-appropriate.

The work programme for meeting each identified need should be drawn up at the end of the analysis. A simple chart is provided for this as an aide-memoire. The work to be done may involve repairing past hurts and deficiencies through therapy, renurturing and reparational activities. (The joint preparation of food can itself be a nurturing experience.) It might involve using some simple techniques to modify behaviour patterns. There may be plans to use food and/or mealtimes to promote the child's identity or self-image. The programme may also have the indirect aim of modifying carer's attitudes or behaviour and establishing new patterns and interactions.

Getting to Grips with a Problem by Analysing Observed Behaviour

....

Child's name   Date of birth   Date of meeting

A The facts

1   Description of the behaviour (give full details).

2   When does it occur?

3   With whom?

4   How often? (calculate frequency by day or week)

5   Where?

6   When, where and how did it start?

7   Is it more or less severe/frequent than at first?

8   What triggers this behaviour?

9   What is the result? (give details of reactions and what actually happens)

10 Does the behaviour vary according to:

   a)   circumstances surrounding the 'meal'?

   b)   the time of day?

   c)   the presence or absence of particular people? If so, who?

Consider: *Do any of the answers to these questions resonate with the child's personal history?*

B Developmental issues

1   Is this behaviour age appropriate? If not, the following points should be raised:

   a)   Is the child a particularly messy eater?

   b)   Does s/he seem to be asking to be fed?

   c)   What sort of food does s/he prefer?

   d)   At what age would this behaviour be more typical?

Consider: *Do the answers to these questions support or challenge other assessments of the age level at which the child is functioning?*

2   Are there known health or developmental problems which have a bearing on this eating problem? e.g.

- cleft palate or other physical deformity

- projectile vomiting as an infant

- mental impairment affecting fine motor development or co-ordination

- sight or hearing problems

- allergies

- sensitivity to food additives

- links betwen certain foods and 'upset tummy', wetting or soiling

- feeding disorder, e.g. anorexia nervosa or bulimia

Consider: *If these conditions have not been explored, should some of them be investigated now?*

C Family history and lifestyle

1   What cultural or religious issues around food or meals are relevant to this child's experience? Are any dietary requirements being acknowledged and met? Is the child being expected to eat unfamiliar food?

2   What role does food play in the child's sense of his/her identity?

3   Does the child expect (from experience) that sweet things are used as rewards or comforters? (NB the role of sweets in access visits may be relevant here).

4   What has been the child's past experience of mealtimes? Is s/he accustomed to sitting down? Using cutlery? Eating with others?

5   What models of eating behaviours has the child had? Were any of these past models appropriate to his/her present living situation?

6   What is the child used to in terms of who eats first? Who eats most? Who serves whom?

Consider: *The place of food in this family and any previous family, and how the child will have experienced it.*

D Issues from the past

1   What was the history of feeding patterns immediately after birth? (NB the importance of feeding in the development of the mother/child relationship)

2   Has the child had experience of being given food as a substitute for real caring, i.e. time and affection?

3   Is there any past pattern of:

  a) compensatory eating?

  b) hoarding?

  c) stealing?

  d) competitive eating

4   Is there any evidence of role confusion in the child's past or present eating patterns? (Meals may be used to play out relationships with parents or siblings)

5   Does the child use food as an emotional weapon, e.g. for rejection, for attention, to buy friendship, to punish parent?

6   Is 'begging' or 'hoarding' outside the home used as a way of showing (or implying) that feeding needs are not being met?

Consider: *the overall place of food in the child's experience of relationships.*

E The root of the problem

On the basis of all this information, what conclusions can be drawn about the underlying problem? Are the eating problems a direct result of other difficulties or deficits (e.g. poor motor co-ordination causing slowness or lack of training resulting in bad table manners?) Or are they an indirect result (e.g. meals are the stage for playing out relationship problems). Or is the child emotionally blocked and functioning at an earlier level of development?

F What should be done?

Using the work programme sheet, list the child's needs in relation to food and mealtimes, the specific suggestions for meeting these needs and who will carry out each task. Indicate the agreed time scale and how progress will be monitored and consider any policy issues and what resources may be needed. Who will support the person carrying out the agreed tasks and how?

Agreed Work Programme for Meeting Each Identified Need

Child's Name ....

Date this programme agreed ....

The need to be met	Suggested work programme (Phased if appropriate)	Support, resource & policy issues & suggested means of dealing with them	Time scale & monitoring	Key people

WHERE DID THE GUIDANCE GO?

A TOOL FOR MANAGERS

Purpose

One of the responsibilities of managers of child care services is to develop and distribute policy, procedure and guidance materials for those who work face to face with children and families. Yet research and inquiries have shown that these essential documents may never reach the practitioners whom they were intended to help. They may be successfully distributed when first issued, but due to the passage of time, staff changes and the lack of efficient storage and retrieval systems in some teams or area offices, they can become lost or forgotten.

The aim of this exercise is to offer a framework for checking out managerial responsibilities in this important area. The scenario is presented in a light-hearted way, but the intention is entirely serious for it might indeed be a matter of life and death. Any manager or managerial group is likely to benefit from taking a few minutes to use this simple tool.

The scenario

An official inquiry is being held because a child for whom your authority has responsibility, has died. You are preparing yourself for the questions that will be asked.

The social worker concerned is newly qualified and was appointed three months ago to a busy child care team. He made a decision which led directly to the tragedy, but which did not comply with your department's policy or procedures or with Dept. of Health regulations and guidance. He claims he did not know of the policy and did not have a copy of the procedure manual. Nor had he heard of the Dept. of Health guidance. At the time of the decision he was without supervision because his team leader was off sick and the area officer was away on a course.

When the inquiry asked the team leader to produce the relevant papers, it emerged that the policy document which covered this issue (distributed two years ago), could not be found, the procedure manual was not entirely up to date and the team leader had never seen the Dept. of Health guidance though she knew of it.

The questions which may be asked by the Inquiry

1 Where are policy documents and procedure manuals supposed to be kept?

2 How many copies of these documents are produced and how are they circulated?

3 What systems are there for updating, monitoring and evaluation?

4 Are all documents numbered and dated? Is their status clear?

5 Are all practitioners given their own copies or easy access to them?

6 How are people instructed about their use?

7 How do you ensure that new staff members know about them?

8 Is legal advice always taken during the production of your department's policy and procedure papers?

9 Is it part of your responsibility to bring Dept. of Health guidance and/or relevant research to the notice of team leaders and practitioners? If so, how do you do this?

10 What are the arrangements for supervision if a regular supervisor is not available?

If you cannot provide satisfactory answers to these questions, do you think that you will be held accountable or negligent by the inquiry?

Some other relevant questions you should ask yourself

1 Are our documents 'user friendly'? How well do they measure up to the standards suggested in the SSI report '*Putting It In Writing*'? For example:

Clarity -	Use of language, e.g. jargon, bureaucratese or generalised meaningless phrases. Or simple, direct and practical?
Accuracy -	Particularly in relation to external references such as legislation or research.
Tone -	Reinforcing rather than undermining the messages which are being communicated.
Style & Size -	Not too long (or too short) to be of practical use.
Presentation -	How effective, how eye-catching is the material?
Overall Impact -	Content, plus the combination of the above factors.

2 When new documents are issued, how much thought is given to ensuring that they will be read, understood and acted upon? Whose responsibility is this?

3 How does your authority plan to involve practitioners and front-line managers in the complete re-write of all departmental child care documents necessitated by new legislation?

MATCHING NEEDS, STRENGTHS AND PLACEMENT RESOURCES
(This exercise is based on material supplied by June Thoburn)

Purpose

Few departments are able to provide an ideal placement for every child. Much more often, a choice must be made between less than ideal alternatives. The object of this exercise is to help staff to find the best possible 'match' between the child's needs and capacities and the available resources. It provides a simple framework for ensuring that needs and strengths will be specified precisely and not just in general terms and that there will be a careful analysis of what a particular placement can offer.

Method

While this exercise can be done by an individual field or residential social worker or by a carer, it is best conducted in a group so that ideas and solutions can be shared. It can be used on training courses of many kinds as a way of sharpening analytical and decision making skills, or it can be an integral part of a case conference or planning meeting.

MATCHING NEEDS, STRENGTHS AND PLACEMENT RESOURCES

(This exercise is based on material supplied by June Thoburn)

The Exercise

Think of a particular child or young person. Then:

1 **Make three lists**

   a) All his or her needs

   b) All his or her strong points

   c) The strong or important relationships which he or she has with family, friends or community

2 **Re-write these lists**, putting them in order of importance of the child's needs.

3 **Write out** a 'job description' for a placement which would meet these needs and enhance or preserve these strengths and relationships. (It can be any type of placement.)

4 **Consider** what the present placement or proposed placement has to offer and weigh it against the 'job description'. Then note:

   a) Which of the child's needs does it *not* meet?

   b) Which of his/her strong points does it *not* cater for?

   c) Which important relationships does it jeopardise?

5 **Consider** whether all or some of these deficits could be made up in some way or will a different placement be necessary? (Take into account the negative impact of a move.)

6 **Write** a detailed plan for the placement specifying what will be done and by whom and covering:

   - placement length
   - family contact
   - work on specific problems
   - education
   - health
   - social development
   - social work and other support for the placement
   - financial support for the placement
   - social work support for the natural family
   - legal status - present and future
   - a leaving care plan

Testing the Evidence
Suggestions for those who chair decision making meetings
(This material is based on ideas supplied by Sue Higginson)

Purpose

This tool is primarily intended for use by those who chair reviews, case conferences and planning meetings at which important decisions must be made. However, the suggestions can be applied by anyone who is involved in decision making. The aim is to reduce misperceptions and unwarranted assumptions and to uncover factual evidence which will support or refute claims and comments. In this way a decision can be arrived at which is based on firm evidence and a balanced understanding of the issues.

If the participants know the chairperson quite well, this may enable them to speak more freely. However, from the chair's point of view, it makes objectivity more difficult and a commitment to testing the evidence will be particularly important. An independent person may more easily spot false assumptions or biases, but will need to be specially alert to the differing priorities and suggestions of members of the group.

Chairing decision-making meetings is a skill which has to be learned, developed and then adapted to specific situations. Although the basic principles remain constant, chairpeople quite properly develop their own personal style. So the methods suggested here are intended to be used creatively to meet particular needs rather than applied routinely or slavishly.

Method

1 Structure the meeting

Advance planning is crucial even if time pressures mean that it has to take place in the few moments just before the meeting begins. The first essential is to clarify the purpose of the gathering and make sure that everyone is in agreement. It is also the responsibility of the chair to make sure that a social history is, or will be, available.

Most meetings fall into three parts:

● information sharing

● discussion of issues/clarification/exploration

● decisions/recommendations/future plans

Without planning, structure and good control from the chair, valuable time is likely to be wasted and important issues may be overlooked or squeezed out. It is worth bearing in mind that if there are 8 or 10 people present, each of them can have only a very short time to speak during each section of the meeting. If essential evidence is to be produced and tested, contributions and discussion need to be as clearly focussed as possible. Introductions may be necessary, but must be brief and time must be allowed for summing up at the end.

2 Identify the issues

Either in preliminary discussion with a few key people, or from written reports, the chair should identify the key issues which will need to be considered. There may be only one issue, but more usually there are three or four. These issues are the heart of the meeting and are the topics about which evidence must be brought out and considered.

3 Check the issues with the participants

Modifications, or additions which are pertinent to the purpose of the meeting should be made. The chair should note relevant facts alongside each issue using single words if possible.

4 Explore each issue in turn

The chair should ask for factual evidence to support or refute each statement. As an aide-memoire, some simple method must be used to indicate the strength of each piece of evidence and whether it is negative or positive in relation to the issue under consideration. The following points will be important:

a) The source of the evidence, e.g. is it direct observation or hearsay?

b) How often the event/problem occurs

c) How long the condition has gone on, e.g. the length of time good care or a good relationship has gone on or when the problem started

d) Are the participants' views unanimous, conflicting or uncertain? What do the parents/caregivers say?

5 The chair's role

In addition to keeping the discussion moving and focussed, the chair should enable participants to produce the evidence which they have in their heads. Until this point, they may not have recognised its significance.

The following techniques are useful:

a) *Challenge*. It is important to ask for examples of behaviour, attitudes etc and to find out whether others in the meeting can confirm important statements or have evidence pointing in a contrary direction. Possible questions include:
    What did s/he actually *do*?
    Could you please describe that to us?
    What effect has this had on the child?
    What makes you think that?

b) *Look for discrepancies and contradictions.* Are the expressed opinions borne out by the evidence?

c) *Look for what might be missing from the whole picture.*

d) *Be alert for racial, cultural, religious or gender stereotyping.* Do the facts fit the description? What effect has been observed in the child?

6 An aide-memoire

Proper minutes are most important but they should not be the responsibility of the chair. However, participants and the chair should take their own notes. These can be extremely brief but must be taken consistently in order to ensure that each issue has been adequately covered and to enable the chair to sum up and present the conclusions succinctly but fully. The example given on the next page is not intended to be a prototype, but is just to show how one chairperson used this very simple method to help her to weigh the evidence and remember the salient points.

TESTING THE EVIDENCE A sample aide-memoire

The scenario

John aged three was the subject of an emergency protection order after a neighbour had phoned the duty officer at 1am and he was found alone, distressed and unwell. The neighbour had also alleged that he was often left alone, had terrible tantrums, was neglected and his mother constantly shouted at him. Mother was found by the police in a night-club. She said her younger sister had promised to come in and look after John. John had been in a foster home for four days. Mother had visited three times.

The purpose of the meeting was to decide whether John should go home or whether a court order should be sought.

This chairperson used the following symbols to identify risk and problems:

risk/problem   ✘   =some evidence   no known risk   ✔   =no evidence

         ✘ ✘ =strong evidence   ✔ ✔ =contrary evidence

Issues

1)	Social history		3)	Neglect? Abuse?
2)	Left unattended?		4)	Tantrums—why?

History

h.v.	Mother 17—wanted baby	✔
s.w.	p.f. visits—mother has other boy-friend	✔
	→ fights	✘
	gr. mo. helpful	✔ ✔
police	no record	✔

Left alone?

police	—no record	✔
s.w.	neighbour seen, says often left	✘ ✘
h.v.	yes but only hearsay	✘
mother	denies. Says her mother comes but now sick	✔

Neglect

h.v.	J. comes clinic. Ears bad	✔
s.w.	flat chaos John ok	✔
g.p.	report ok	✔
foster m.	child fine	✔ ✔

Tantrums

h.v.	Yes. seen. Severe	✘
mother	Yes often	✘
f. mother	No. Child deaf	✔
Medical adviser	'glue ear'	✔ ✔

Name Index

Printed in the United Kingdom for HMSO
Dd299956 9/94 C10 G3397 10170